Information and Communication Technology

KEY STAGE 2:
YEAR 5
PRIMARY 6

Frances Mackay

HOPSCOTCH
EDUCATIONAL PUBLISHING

Contents

◆ ABOUT THE SERIES ◆

Developing ICT Skills is a series of books written specifically to complement the QCA and DfEE *Information Technology Scheme of Work for Key Stages 1 and 2*. There is one book for each year from Reception/Year 1 (Scottish Primary 1/2), through Key Stage 1 to Year 6 (Scottish Primary 7) at the end of Key Stage 2.

The series offers a structured approach with the non-specialist in mind and provides detailed lesson plans to teach specific ICT skills. A unique feature of the series is the provision of differentiated photocopiable activities designed to support each lesson. Most of these activities are independent tasks that can be completed away from the computer or ICT equipment being used, thereby enabling the teacher to work with a focus group at the computer. The differentiation of the activities considerably reduces teacher preparation time when planning group work.

The lessons have been specifically written for the classroom with access to only one computer but will, of course, work equally well in a computer suite situation.

Accompanying each of the two books for Key Stage 1 is a CD-Rom, produced by AirCom International, that contains activities designed to support each lesson. The school will not, therefore, need a separate word-processor, art or music package, for example, to teach the ICT skills being addressed. If schools prefer to use their own computer programs, however, each book is designed to stand alone without the accompanying CD-Rom.

◆ ABOUT THIS BOOK ◆

This book is for teachers of Year 5 (Scottish Primary level 6) children. It aims to:
◆ develop children's ICT skills through a series of structured lessons aimed at increasing children's awareness of the strengths and limitations of ICT;

◆ support teachers by providing practical teaching methods and activity ideas based on whole class, group, paired and individual teaching;

◆ support non-specialist teachers by providing structured lesson plans with practical ideas and 'specialist tips' designed to address some of the common problems the children (and teachers!) may experience;

◆ provide lessons that are cross-curricular wherever possible;

◆ encourage the children to recognise the importance of ICT in everyday experiences;

◆ encourage enjoyment as well as confidence in using ICT skills.

◆ LESSON CONTENT ◆

◆ Learning objectives

This sets out the specific learning objectives for each lesson.

◆ Resources

This is a list of what you will need to do the lessons.

◆ Whole class introduction

This provides ideas for introducing the activity, and may include key questions to ask the children, so that they can move on to their group task having learned the concepts and the vocabulary they will need for the group activities.

◆ Group activities

Focus group – with the teacher
This follows the whole class introduction and is a teaching session with the teacher working together with the children at the computer (or other ICT equipment). The teaching in this session can either be carried out with the class as a whole (by using a computer and a projected screen or by using a computer suite) or within a small group while the rest of the class do the photocopiable activity sheets (if appropriate) or another (sometimes related) independent task. This section contains suggestions for teaching the key concepts and skills relating directly to the ICT learning objectives for the lesson. Hints and tips are provided to help support the teacher when introducing these skills.

Using the photocopiable activity sheets
The activity sheets provide three activities that can be done more or less independently from the teacher. These sheets are differentiated so that the same task can be completed by below average, average and above average children at their own level. Activity sheet 1 tasks are the easiest and Activity sheet 3 the hardest. In most cases, the sheets contain tasks that are designed to be completed away from the computer or ICT equipment being used but reinforce the skills that will be used at the computer itself. Many activities are also designed so the children can compare a manual task with a computer one (editing text, for example), thereby enabling a discussion during the plenary session about the strengths and limitations of ICT.

Sometimes, the sheets can be completed immediately after the whole class introduction (so some children may be working with the teacher in a small group at the computer while the rest are completing the sheets). At other times, the sheets are to be completed only after the children have experienced the focus group session. (In a classroom with only one computer then, the children may need to be set other independent tasks until they have been part of the focus group.)

For each lesson then, each child should experience the whole class introduction and a focus group session as well as completing an activity sheet. In classrooms with only one computer this means the teacher may need to organise the lesson over a week, for example:

Mon	whole class introduction
	group A – with the teacher at computer (focus group session)
	groups B, C and D – completing activity sheets
Tues	group B – focus group session
	group A – activity sheet
	groups C and D – independent tasks
Wed	group C – focus group session
	groups A, B and D – independent tasks
Thurs	group D – focus group session
	groups A, B and C – independent tasks
	plenary – all groups

◆ Plenary session

This suggests ideas for a whole-class review to discuss the learning outcomes, and gives questions to ask so that the children have a chance to reflect on what they have learned and for the teacher to assess their knowledge and understanding. This session may not necessarily take place on the same day as the whole class introduction - it may come at the end of the week after all the children have completed their focus group session and activity sheets.

APPENDIX

At the back of this book are some extra photocopiable pages. Page 62 offers suggestions for how these pages could be used. Most of the pages have been prepared for the teacher to use as resources for particular lessons but there are also ideas on how to use the pages to develop further activities in follow-up sessions. Where relevant, these pages also contain the answers to particular activity sheets.

Page 72 is an assessment sheet that outlines the basic concepts and skills that a Year 5/P6 child should experience. The teacher can photocopy this page for each child and, together with the work produced from each lesson, use it to compile a comprehensive individual ICT profile to make assessments and determine future targets.

HARDWARE REQUIREMENTS

Teachers using this book will require a Windows-based multi-media computer and colour printer, calculators, a control box and simple switches and output devices such as buzzers, lights and small motors.

SOFTWARE REQUIREMENTS

The following software is required:
◆ an object-based drawing package;
◆ data-handling software that uses logical operators including 'AND' and 'OR' for searching data;
◆ an American CD-Rom encyclopaedia;
◆ Internet access (optional);
◆ spreadsheet software.

If you do not have all the software listed, contact your LEA for a recommended software toolbox. They may also provide technical support and training. Alternatively, contact Granada Learning on 0161 827 2927 (Blackcat Toolbox) or Logotron on 01223 425558.

TEACHING ICT

For many of today's adults there has always been a degree of mystique surrounding ICT skills. Some people have even avoided contact with computers altogether! However, in the teaching profession, this is not an option. In truth, there is nothing difficult about acquiring or teaching ICT and, in fact, there has never been a better or more exciting time to become a computer user. To become a confident ICT user, whether teacher or pupil, you need to be taught a few basic skills and to become familiar with the way technology works, but you do not need to become an expert. The National Curriculum requires ICT to be taught to all pupils and this can seem daunting if the teacher is learning alongside the pupils. In this series we aim to provide the teacher with the materials, skills and knowledge that will make covering the ICT Scheme of Work an achievable and positive experience. We expect children who take part in the lessons to learn age-appropriate ICT skills and to become discerning users of technology.

Schools that teach ICT skills discretely then transfer those skills to other subject areas find that children achieve higher levels of ICT competence than when ICT skills are taught **only** through other subjects. This suggests that teachers should set aside time specifically for the teaching of ICT skills. This does not mean that it is necessary to timetable ICT lessons every week but it is important to make sure some ICT lessons are devoted to the teaching of specific ICT skills. This can be carried out through occasional whole-class lessons as well as small group or individual lessons and does not necessarily require the whole class to be working on ICT at the same time. The lessons in this book agree with this premise and ICT is the main focus of each one. However, where there are opportunities for links with other curriculum areas, advantage of this has been taken.

Prior to the publication of the QCA and DfEE IT SoW it was difficult for schools to know exactly what ICT skills should be taught to each year group. We have now been presented with a clear and comprehensive guide which clearly demonstrates continuity and progression. If you are working with older children who have not had the opportunity to acquire the rudimentary skills, it would be best to work at the correct level for these children. Hence the years and levels suggested in the IT SoW and in this series of books are to be taken as desirable guidelines.

In order to achieve a high level of success for the children, teaching intentions should be very clear and built within a whole-school scheme of work that demonstrates evident continuity and progression of concepts and skills. This is extremely important in ICT because today, perhaps more than ever before, children vary considerably in their ICT capabilities. Many children who have access to ICT outside school can appear to have greater skills in handling software and hardware but teachers need to be aware that these children may not necessarily have the full range of ICT capabilities expected of them in the programmes of study. Regular observations and assessments are therefore necessary to ascertain the best tasks and experiences to support the children's learning.

Reliability of the technology has often been one of the biggest hurdles for schools! Therefore, before you begin to use the lessons in this series, we recommend that you check that all the necessary equipment is working correctly. Access to only broken or out-of-date technology is time wasting and very frustrating for teachers and children alike.

Published by Hopscotch Educational Publishing Ltd, Althorpe House, Althorpe Street, Leamington Spa CV31 2AU Tel: 01926 744227

© 2000 Hopscotch Educational Publishing

Written by Frances Mackay
Series consultant – Ayleen Driver
Series design by Blade Communications
Illustrated by Susan Hutchison
Cover illustration by Susan Hutchison
Printed by Clintplan, Southam

Frances Mackay hereby asserts her moral right to be identified as the author of this work in accordance with the Copyright, Designs and Patents Act, 1988.

ISBN 1-902239-45-8

Lesson 1

Manipulating shapes

 Learning objectives

✦ To understand that designs can be created by combining and manipulating shapes.
✦ To understand that ICT can be used to combine and manipulate shapes.
✦ To move, rotate and resize graphic elements in an object-based drawing package.

 Resources

✦ Photocopiable page 63.
✦ Pictures of abstract art that uses geometric shapes, such as 'The Snail' by Henri Matisse or 'Swinging' by Wassily Kandinsky.
✦ An object-based drawing package or art package.

 Whole class introduction

✦ Share the abstract art pictures. Talk about how the artists have used different shapes and colours to create their designs. Explain that by using collage the artist can overlap shapes to create a layered effect or to 'mix' colours. Discuss any recent collages the children may have done themselves to compare techniques and results.
✦ Discuss the geometric shapes in the pictures – can the children name them? Share the picture on photocopiable page 63. Explain that this design has been created using pentagons (some with circles). How have the shapes been arranged on the page? Discuss how the positioning of the shapes has been changed by translating, rotating, reflecting, enlarging and reducing them. Use the examples at the bottom of page 63 to explain these terms. Relate this to work the children may have done in maths. Explain that by using collage the artist is able to cut out shapes and position them in a variety of different ways on the page before deciding on their final position.
✦ Tell the children that they are going to experiment with manipulating shapes to make a collage using an activity sheet as well as a computer program.

 Group activities

Focus group – with the teacher

✦ Remind the children about the work they have done before using art packages. Discuss how it can be quite laborious and time-consuming using these packages to move specific objects within a drawing (when creating an abstract design like the pictures they looked at earlier, for example). Explain that an object-based drawing package has been specifically designed to do these kinds of tasks and shapes can be selected and rearranged, resized, copied and layered more easily.
✦ Demonstrate how to select, rotate and resize geometric shapes in the package as well as how to change the colours of the shapes. Ask the children to work in pairs to use these techniques to create different images, print out their work and compare the results.

Using the photocopiable activity sheets

✦ Use the activity sheets before or after the computer program. Remind them about rotating, translating, reflecting and overlapping to create different effects. Tissue paper can be used to simulate colour-mixing by overlapping layers.

 Plenary session

Share the activity sheet collages. Did the children rotate, translate and overlap their shapes? What effects did this create? Was it possible to create different colours by overlapping? Ask someone using Activity sheet 3 to explain how they resized their shape using the graph paper. Compare this work with the computer activity. Did the computer make it easier or more difficult to create a collage? Was it easier to resize a shape, for example? How easy was it to change a colour? What advantages and disadvantages are there in using the computer to do this task? Which final result are they most pleased with? Why? What other uses can they suggest for this program?

ICT Skills

✦ Making a collage ✦

✦ Trace the shape below onto card. Cut it out. Use it as a template to cut out different coloured paper. Arrange the cut-outs on the page to make a collage. Glue the shapes in place when you are happy with your design.

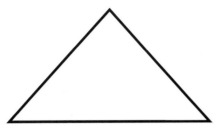

✦ Make your collage here.

✦ Making a collage ✦

✦ Trace the shapes below onto card. Use them as templates to cut out different coloured paper. Arrange the cut-outs on the page to make a collage. Glue the shapes in place when you are happy with your design.

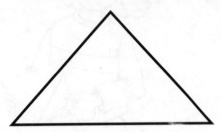
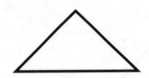

✦ Make your collage here.

Photocopiable
©Hopscotch Educational Publishing

✦ Making a collage ✦

✦ Resize the shape below by using the graph paper to make it
twice as large. Then re-size the new shape to twice its size.
Trace the three shapes onto card and cut them out. Use the
shapes as templates to cut out different coloured paper.
Arrange the cut-outs in the space below to make a collage.
Glue the shapes in place when you are happy with your design.

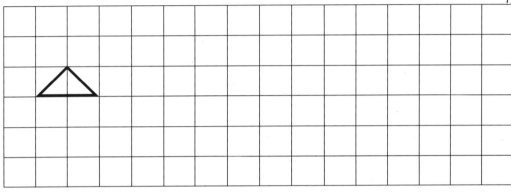

✦ Make your collage here.

Lesson 2

Creating plans

Learning objectives

✦ To understand that plans are scaled representations of the real world.
✦ To draw a plan.
✦ To understand that ICT can be used to create plans.
✦ To create and manipulate objects using geometric tools in an object-based graphics package.

Resources

✦ Photocopiable page 64.
✦ House or kitchen design plans.
✦ An object-based drawing package or art package.

Whole class introduction

✦ Tell the children they will be looking at house plans. Has anyone seen or used a house plan before? Why is it necessary to have a plan? How are they used and for what purpose? What is special about such plans? (Discuss how they show a view of something from the top as if the roof of the house had been lifted off and you are looking straight down on the objects below.)
✦ Show the children the house or kitchen plan. Discuss how it is presented, what it represents and who may want to use it. What skills do they think they might need in order to understand the plan? (Refer to any key to symbols and scales, for example.)
✦ Look at some of the objects in the plan. Remind them how they show a top view. Use page 64 to demonstrate this. Discuss how each of the pictured pieces of kitchen furniture, the walls, doors and windows are represented in the plan.
✦ Tell the children that they are going to draw their own plans using an activity sheet and a computer program.

Group activities

Focus group – with the teacher

✦ Remind the children how they used an object-based graphics package or art package to create an abstract design in Lesson 1. Tell them that the program can also be used to create their own shapes. Show them how to create various shapes that could be used in a plan – a round table, a square table, a curved chair and so on.
✦ Challenge them to create their own symbols and then draw a plan of their classroom.
✦ More able children could be encouraged to work to scale.

Using the photocopiable activity sheets

✦ The activity sheets could be used before or after the computer session.

Plenary session

Share the activity sheet plans. What difficulties did the children have in drawing the plan or designing the symbols? How did this manual task compare with the computer task? Which activity (activity sheet or computer) enabled them to manipulate the objects more easily? What are the advantages and disadvantages of using a computer program to do plans? Which end product were they most pleased with? Why? What sort of businesses might use a program such as this?

©Hopscotch Educational Publishing
ICT Skills

✦ Living room plan ✦

✦ Complete the plan below of a living room by using the following symbols.

chair

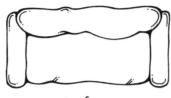
sofa

coffee table

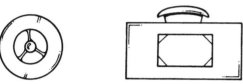

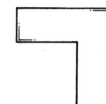

lamp   desk and chair   television   small table   book case

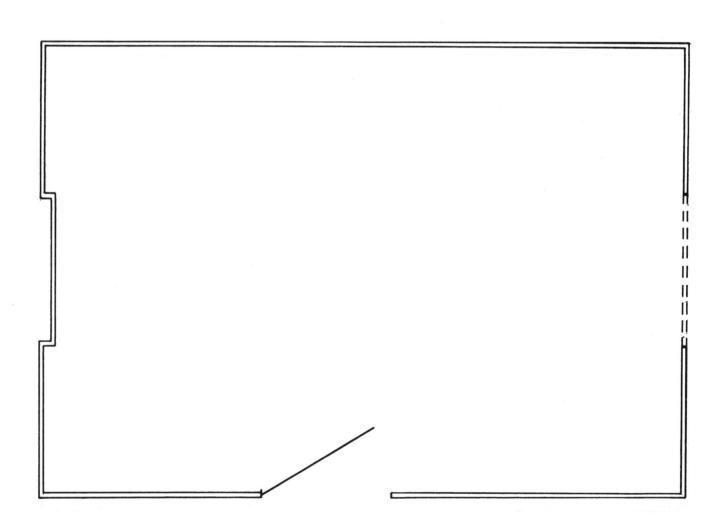

✦ Living room plan ✦

✦ Complete the plan below of a living room by inventing symbols for the items below. The first ones have been done for you.

chair

lamp

desk and chair

television

sofa

round coffee table

small table

hi-fi

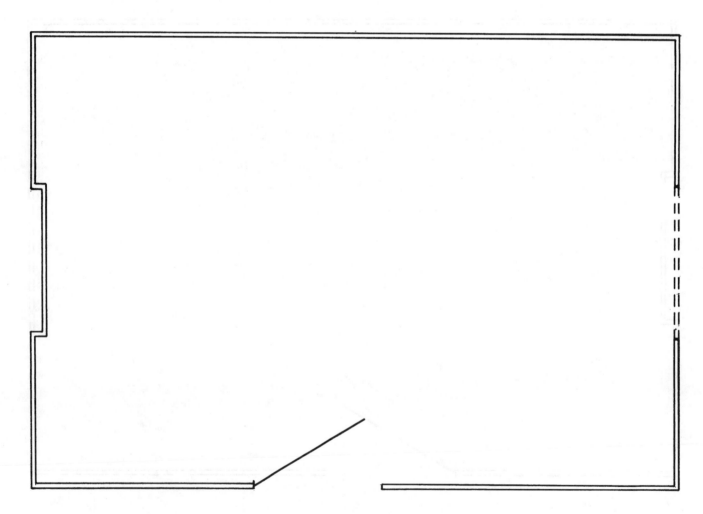

✦ Living room plan ✦

✦ Invent a symbol for each item below. Draw the symbol next to each word in the box. One has been done for you.

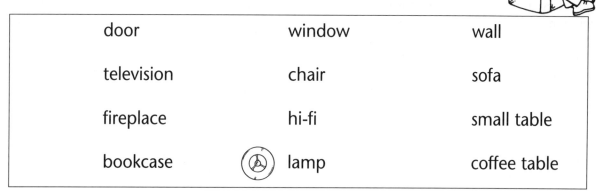

door	window	wall
television	chair	sofa
fireplace	hi-fi	small table
bookcase	⊛ lamp	coffee table

✦ Now use these symbols to draw a plan of a living room in the space below.

Lesson 3

Searching databases – 1

 Learning objectives

♦ To understand that collecting and storing information in an organised way helps us find specific information.
♦ To know that data records consist of fields into which data is entered.
♦ To search a database using 'more than', 'less than' and 'including'.

 Resources

♦ Photocopiable page 65.
♦ Data-handling software that uses logical operators including 'AND' and 'OR' for searching data.
♦ A prepared database, for example planets in the solar system.

 Whole class introduction

♦ Before the lesson, photocopy page 65 and cut out the individual record cards so that each child has one card. Tell them that they will be using a database computer program and remind them how these programs are based on information gathered in the form of records. Can they recall using record cards before? Remind them how record cards contain a lot of different information about something and that this information is divided into separate headings, or fields.
♦ Provide each child with a record card from page 65. Tell them that these records have been designed to contain information about themselves. Ask them to complete the cards. Note: for hair colour, have a list of key words for them to choose from (include 'light brown' and 'dark brown').
♦ Explain that if all the cards were put together they would form a file – just like cards in a filing cabinet – and if we wanted to find information about the children in the file, we would have to search through the records. Explain that the information on the cards is presented in different ways – as a number (for example, age), as words (for example, eye colour) or as a choice (for example, do you play sport?).

♦ Prepare the children for the activity sheets and the computer program by carrying out simple searches using the cards. Ask them to stand up in response to various questions, such as 'How many children have blue eyes?', 'How many children have more than two brothers and sisters?', 'How many children are less than ten years old?' and 'How many children have a hair colour that includes brown?'

 Group activities

Focus group – with the teacher

♦ Explain how a computer database can contain information just like the record cards. Remind the children how they had to search through their paper records to find the answers to questions. Tell them that the computer program is designed to do this much more quickly. Demonstrate how to enter the program and select the database you want to use. Show them how to use '=<' and '=>' in a search. Note: You may prefer to use the same information as on the activity sheet cards. The children could then race the computer to find answers. Ask them to answer a set of comparative questions such as: 'Compare the number of moons of Mars, Jupiter and Saturn.' If possible, invite the children to compare the database search with a search using the Internet.

Using the photocopiable activity sheets

♦ The children should complete the activity sheets before the computer session.

 Plenary session

Share the responses to the activity sheets. What difficulties did they have? Compare using the CD-Rom (and Internet) with the printed activity sheet source. What advantages/disadvantages are there of each source? Which one would be the most reliable/up-to-date? Which search takes the least time? Which search provides us with more information?

✦ The planets ✦

✦ Use these record cards to answer the questions below.

name: Mercury **diameter:** 4 878km **av. distance from Sun:** 57 900 100km **rotation time:** 84 450 min **length of year:** 88 days **rings:** no **moons:** 0 **atmosphere:** none	**name:** Venus **diameter:** 12 104km **av. distance from Sun:** 108 200 600km **rotation time:** 349 952 min **length of year:** 225 days **rings:** no **moons:** 0 **atmosphere:** carbon dioxide	**name:** Earth **diameter:** 12 756km **av. distance from Sun:** 149 600 000km **rotation time:** 1 436 min **length of year:** 365.25 days **rings:** no **moons:** 1 **atmosphere:** nitrogen, oxygen
name: Mars **diameter:** 6 794km **av. distance from Sun:** 227 900 000km **rotation time:** 1 477 min **length of year:** 687 days **rings:** no **moons:** 2 **atmosphere:** carbon dioxide	**name:** Jupiter **diameter:** 142 984km **av. distance from Sun:** 778 300 000km **rotation time:** 590 min **length of year:** 4 332 days **rings:** yes **moons:** 16 **atmosphere:** hydrogen, helium	**name:** Saturn **diameter:** 120 600km **av. distance from Sun:** 1 427 000 000km **rotation time:** 623 min **length of year:** 10 759 days **rings:** yes **moons:** 21 **atmosphere:** hydrogen, helium
name: Uranus **diameter:** 51 118km **av. distance from Sun:** 2 869 600 000km **rotation time:** 1 034 min **length of year:** 30 685 days **rings:** yes **moons:** 15 **atmosphere:** hydrogen, helium, methane	**name:** Neptune **diameter:** 50 000km **av. distance from Sun:** 4 496 700 000km **rotation time:** 1 140 min **length of year:** 60 189 days **rings:** yes **moons:** 8 **atmosphere:** hydrogen, helium, methane	**name:** Pluto **diameter:** 2 290km **av. distance from Sun:** 5 913 490 000km **rotation time:** 9 198 min **length of year:** 90 777 days **rings:** no **moons:** 1 **atmosphere:** none

✦ Tick the correct answer.

1. How many records are on this page?   9 ☐   8 ☐

2. How many fields are on each record?   9 ☐   8 ☐

3. Which planet has more than 20 moons?   Uranus ☐   Saturn ☐

4. Which planet is less than 3000km in diameter?   Venus ☐   Pluto ☐

5. Which planets have rings?   Mars, Venus, Pluto and Mercury ☐

    Jupiter, Saturn, Uranus and Neptune ☐

6. Which planets are less than 200 000 000km from the Sun?

    Mars, Uranus and Pluto ☐

    Earth, Venus and Mercury ☐

✦ The planets ✦

✦ Use these record cards to answer the questions below.

name: Mercury **diameter:** 4 878km **av. distance from Sun:** 57 900 100km **rotation time:** 84 450 min **length of year:** 88 days **rings:** no **moons:** 0 **atmosphere:** none	**name:** Venus **diameter:** 12 104km **av. distance from Sun:** 108 200 600km **rotation time:** 349 952 min **length of year:** 225 days **rings:** no **moons:** 0 **atmosphere:** carbon dioxide	**name:** Earth **diameter:** 12 756km **av. distance from Sun:** 149 600 000km **rotation time:** 1 436 min **length of year:** 365.25 days **rings:** no **moons:** 1 **atmosphere:** nitrogen, oxygen
name: Mars **diameter:** 6 794km **av. distance from Sun:** 227 900 000km **rotation time:** 1 477 min **length of year:** 687 days **rings:** no **moons:** 2 **atmosphere:** carbon dioxide	**name:** Jupiter **diameter:** 142 984km **av. distance from Sun:** 778 300 000km **rotation time:** 590 min **length of year:** 4 332 days **rings:** yes **moons:** 16 **atmosphere:** hydrogen, helium	**name:** Saturn **diameter:** 120 600km **av. distance from Sun:** 1 427 000 000km **rotation time:** 623 min **length of year:** 10 759 days **rings:** yes **moons:** 21 **atmosphere:** hydrogen, helium
name: Uranus **diameter:** 51 118km **av. distance from Sun:** 2 869 600 000km **rotation time:** 1 034 min **length of year:** 30 685 days **rings:** yes **moons:** 15 **atmosphere:** hydrogen, helium, methane	**name:** Neptune **diameter:** 50 000km **av. distance from Sun:** 4 496 700 000km **rotation time:** 1 140 min **length of year:** 60 189 days **rings:** yes **moons:** 8 **atmosphere:** hydrogen, helium, methane	**name:** Pluto **diameter:** 2 290km **av. distance from Sun:** 5 913 490 000km **rotation time:** 9 198 min **length of year:** 90 777 days **rings:** no **moons:** 1 **atmosphere:** none

1. How many records are on this page?_____

2. How many fields are on each record?_____

3. Which planets have more than 7 moons?_____

4. Which planets are less than 7000km in diameter?_____

    _____

5. Which planets have an atmosphere that includes methane?_____

6. Which planets are less than 200 000 000km from the Sun?_____

    _____

✦ The planets ✦

✦ Use these record cards to answer the questions below.

name: Mercury **diameter:** 4 878km **av. distance from Sun:** 57 900 100km **rotation time:** 84 450 min **length of year:** 88 days **rings:** no **moons:** 0 **atmosphere:** none	**name:** Venus **diameter:** 12 104km **av. distance from Sun:** 108 200 600km **rotation time:** 349 952 min **length of year:** 225 days **rings:** no **moons:** 0 **atmosphere:** carbon dioxide	**name:** Earth **diameter:** 12 756km **av. distance from Sun:** 149 600 000km **rotation time:** 1 436 min **length of year:** 365.25 days **rings:** no **moons:** 1 **atmosphere:** nitrogen, oxygen
name: Mars **diameter:** 6 794km **av. distance from Sun:** 227 900 000km **rotation time:** 1 477 min **length of year:** 687 days **rings:** no **moons:** 2 **atmosphere:** carbon dioxide	**name:** Jupiter **diameter:** 142 984km **av. distance from Sun:** 778 300 000km **rotation time:** 590 min **length of year:** 4 332 days **rings:** yes **moons:** 16 **atmosphere:** hydrogen, helium	**name:** Saturn **diameter:** 120 600km **av. distance from Sun:** 1 427 000 000km **rotation time:** 623 min **length of year:** 10 759 days **rings:** yes **moons:** 21 **atmosphere:** hydrogen, helium
name: Uranus **diameter:** 51 118km **av. distance from Sun:** 2 869 600 000km **rotation time:** 1 034 min **length of year:** 30 685 days **rings:** yes **moons:** 15 **atmosphere:** hydrogen, helium, methane	**name:** Neptune **diameter:** 50 000km **av. distance from Sun:** 4 496 700 000km **rotation time:** 1 140 min **length of year:** 60 189 days **rings:** yes **moons:** 8 **atmosphere:** hydrogen, helium, methane	**name:** Pluto **diameter:** 2 290km **av. distance from Sun:** 5 913 490 000km **rotation time:** 9 198 min **length of year:** 90 777 days **rings:** no **moons:** 1 **atmosphere:** none

1. List the fields on each record _____

     _____

2. Which planets have an atmosphere that includes hydrogen?_____

     _____

3. Which planets have a rotation time of less than 1440 min?_____

     _____

4. Which planets are more than 230 000 000km from the Sun?_____

     _____

Lesson 4

Searching databases – 2

 ### Learning objectives

+ To understand that information can be searched using more than one criterion.
+ To search a database using 'AND'.
+ To use ICT to test an hypothesis.
+ To understand and interpret a scatter/line graph.

 ### Resources

+ Photocopiable page 66.
+ Data-handling software that uses logical operators including 'AND' and 'OR' for searching data.
+ A prepared database, for example birds.

 ### Whole class introduction

+ Before the lesson enlarge photocopiable page 66. Cut the page in half to separate the record cards from the graph.
+ Remind the children about the work they carried out searching a database in Lesson 3. Tell them that they will be learning about another way to search a database, using the word 'AND'. Explain that in using 'AND' they will be considering more than one field on the records. Carry out a simple activity to illustrate this. For example, ask the children to think about what they had for breakfast this morning and supper last night. Ask them to put up their hands or stand up in response to your questions: 'Who had toast for breakfast?', 'Who had hot chocolate for supper?', 'Who had cereal for breakfast?', 'Who had toast for supper?' Then, 'Who had toast for breakfast **AND** hot chocolate for supper?' 'Who had cereal for breakfast **AND** no supper?' and so on.
+ Share the record cards on page 66. Revise the type of searches carried out in Lesson 3 by asking questions such as 'Which birds have a wingspan of more than 20cm?', 'Which birds have a body length less than 20cm?', 'Which birds have a feather colour that includes white?'
+ Then introduce the 'AND' type questions: 'Which birds live on the land AND build nests on cliffs?',

'Which birds are white in colour AND lay white eggs?' Challenge the children to look at the records and tell you their own 'AND' type questions. Ask them to check the answers by searching on each criterion separately.
+ Now explain how we can use data to test out an idea or hypothesis – to see if there are any relationships in the data. As an example, ask them to look at the wingspan and body length fields of the records. Can they notice anything about the measurements? Do the birds with a longer body length have a wider wingspan? Share the graph on page 66. Explain how the wingspans and body lengths of each bird on the records have been plotted. What do they notice? Tell them that a computer database can plot graphs for us to help us look for evidence to prove or disprove an hypothesis.

 ### Group activities

Focus group – with the teacher

+ Show the children how to carry out an 'AND' search using the prepared database. Ask them to work as a group to formulate 'AND' questions to search. Ask them to check their answers by searching on each criterion separately. You could give them an hypothesis to prove or disprove, such as 'the smaller the bird, the more eggs it lays'. Ask them to print out graphs to support their conclusions.

Using the photocopiable activity sheets

+ Use the activity sheets before the computer session.

 ### Plenary session

Share responses to the activity sheets. What difficulties were there? Compare this paper search with the computer one. What differences are there? Which search is more accurate/reliable? Discuss any hypotheses that were tested and the resulting graphs.

©Hopscotch Educational Publishing

✦ Birds ✦

✦ Use these record cards to answer the questions below.

name: storm petrel	1
land/sea: sea
colour: black, white
food: small sea animals and fish
wingspan: 12cm – **body length:** 15cm
egg colour: white, red specks
max no. of eggs laid: 1
nest site: rocks or grass

name: sparrowhawk	2
land/sea: land
colour: brown, grey
food: birds, mice, frogs, insects
wingspan: 23cm – **body length:** 38cm
egg colour: blue-white, red splashes
max no. of eggs laid: 6
nest site: trees

name: tawny owl	3
land/sea: land
colour: brown
food: small mammals, birds, insects
wingspan: 25cm – **body length:** 38cm
egg colour: white
max no. of eggs laid: 4
nest site: hollow trees

name: swift	4
land/sea: land
colour: black
food: insects
wingspan: 17cm – **body length:** 18cm
egg colour: white
max no. of eggs laid: 3
nest site: house eaves, cliffs

name: green woodpecker	5
land/sea: land
colour: green
food: insects
wingspan: 16cm – **body length:** 32cm
egg colour: white
max no. of eggs laid: 7
nest site: holes in trees

name: blackbird	6
land/sea: land
colour: black
food: worms, insects, fruit, seeds
wingspan: 13cm – **body length:** 25cm
egg colour: green-white, red blotches
max no. of eggs laid: 6
nest site: bushes, hedges, trees

name: chaffinch	7
land/sea: land
colour: many
food: insects, seeds, fruit
wingspan: 9cm – **body length:** 15cm
egg colour: reddish brown, black
max no. of eggs laid: 6
nest site: hedges, trees

name: magpie	8
land/sea: land
colour: black, white
food: eggs, small mammals, insects
wingspan: 19cm – **body length:** 46cm
egg colour: blue-green, brown spots
max no. of eggs laid: 8
nest site: trees

name: gannet	9
land/sea: sea
colour: white, little buff and black
food: fish
wingspan: 48cm – **body length:** 90cm
egg colour: blue-green
max no. of eggs laid: 1
nest site: cliffs

✦ Tick the correct answers.

1. Which birds are sea birds AND lay 1 egg?   swift, magpie ☐   gannet, petrel ☐

2. Which bird is black AND lays white eggs?   swift ☐   magpie ☐

3. Which birds lay 6 eggs AND nest in trees?   tawny owl, swift, gannet ☐

    sparrowhawk, blackbird, chaffinch ☐

4. Which birds have a wingspan over 20cm AND a body length over 30cm ?

    tawny owl, gannet, sparrowhawk ☐

    woodpecker, swift, blackbird ☐

✦ Write your own 'AND' question about these records.

_____

ICT Skills

Photocopiable
©Hopscotch Educational Publishing

✦ Birds ✦

✦ Use these record cards to answer the questions below.

name: storm petrel 1 **land/sea:** sea **colour:** black, white **food:** small sea animals and fish **wingspan:** 12cm – **body length:** 15cm **egg colour:** white, red specks **max no. of eggs laid:** 1 **nest site:** rocks or grass	**name:** sparrowhawk 2 **land/sea:** land **colour:** brown, grey **food:** birds, mice, frogs, insects **wingspan:** 23cm – **body length:** 38cm **egg colour:** blue-white, red splashes **max no. of eggs laid:** 6 **nest site:** trees	**name:** tawny owl 3 **land/sea:** land **colour:** brown **food:** small mammals, birds, insects **wingspan:** 25cm – **body length:** 38cm **egg colour:** white **max no. of eggs laid:** 4 **nest site:** hollow trees
name: swift 4 **land/sea:** land **colour:** black **food:** insects **wingspan:** 17cm – **body length:** 18cm **egg colour:** white **max no. of eggs laid:** 3 **nest site:** house eaves, cliffs	**name:** green woodpecker 5 **land/sea:** land **colour:** green **food:** insects **wingspan:** 16cm – **body length:** 32cm **egg colour:** white **max no. of eggs laid:** 7 **nest site:** holes in trees	**name:** blackbird 6 **land/sea:** land **colour:** black **food:** worms, insects, fruit, seeds **wingspan:** 13cm – **body length:** 25cm **egg colour:** green-white, red blotches **max no. of eggs laid:** 6 **nest site:** bushes, hedges, trees
name: chaffinch 7 **land/sea:** land **colour:** many **food:** insects, seeds, fruit **wingspan:** 9cm – **body length:** 15cm **egg colour:** reddish brown, black **max no. of eggs laid:** 6 **nest site:** hedges, trees	**name:** magpie 8 **land/sea:** land **colour:** black, white **food:** eggs, small mammals, insects **wingspan:** 19cm – **body length:** 46cm **egg colour:** blue-green, brown spots **max no. of eggs laid:** 8 **nest site:** trees	**name:** gannet 9 **land/sea:** sea **colour:** white, little buff and black **food:** fish **wingspan:** 48cm – **body length:** 90cm **egg colour:** blue-green **max no. of eggs laid:** 1 **nest site:** cliffs

1. Which birds are sea birds AND lay 1 egg?_____

2. Which bird is black AND lays white eggs?_____

3. Which birds lay 6 eggs AND nest in trees?_____

4. Which birds have a wingspan over 20 cm AND a body length over 30 cm ?

   _____

5. Which birds eat insects AND nest in trees?_____

   _____

✦ On the back of this sheet write two of your own 'AND' questions about these records.

✦ Birds ✦

✦ Use these record cards to answer the questions below.

name: storm petrel ☐1 **land/sea:** sea **colour:** black, white **food:** small sea animals and fish **wingspan:** 12cm – **body length:** 15cm **egg colour:** white, red specks **max no. of eggs laid:** 1 **nest site:** rocks or grass	

name: storm petrel ☐1
land/sea: sea
colour: black, white
food: small sea animals and fish
wingspan: 12cm – **body length:** 15cm
egg colour: white, red specks
max no. of eggs laid: 1
nest site: rocks or grass

name: sparrowhawk ☐2
land/sea: land
colour: brown, grey
food: birds, mice, frogs, insects
wingspan: 23cm – **body length:** 38cm
egg colour: blue-white, red splashes
max no. of eggs laid: 6
nest site: trees

name: tawny owl ☐3
land/sea: land
colour: brown
food: small mammals, birds, insects
wingspan: 25cm – **body length:** 38cm
egg colour: white
max no. of eggs laid: 4
nest site: hollow trees

name: swift ☐4
land/sea: land
colour: black
food: insects
wingspan: 17cm – **body length:** 18cm
egg colour: white
max no. of eggs laid: 3
nest site: house eaves, cliffs

name: green woodpecker ☐5
land/sea: land
colour: green
food: insects
wingspan: 16cm – **body length:** 32cm
egg colour: white
max no. of eggs laid: 7
nest site: holes in trees

name: blackbird ☐6
land/sea: land
colour: black
food: worms, insects, fruit, seeds
wingspan: 13cm – **body length:** 25cm
egg colour: green-white, red blotches
max no. of eggs laid: 6
nest site: bushes, hedges, trees

name: chaffinch ☐7
land/sea: land
colour: many
food: insects, seeds, fruit
wingspan: 9cm – **body length:** 15cm
egg colour: reddish brown, black
max no. of eggs laid: 6
nest site: hedges, trees

name: magpie ☐8
land/sea: land
colour: black, white
food: eggs, small mammals, insects
wingspan: 19cm – **body length:** 46cm
egg colour: blue-green, brown spots
max no. of eggs laid: 8
nest site: trees

name: gannet ☐9
land/sea: sea
colour: white, little buff and black
food: fish
wingspan: 48cm – **body length:** 90cm
egg colour: blue-green
max no. of eggs laid: 1
nest site: cliffs

1. Which birds only eat insects AND lay white eggs?_____

2. Which birds have a wingspan less than 20 cm AND a body length less than 20cm?
   _____

3. Which birds lay less than 7 eggs AND nest in trees?_____
   _____

4. Which birds lay more than 4 eggs AND lay white eggs?_____

5. Which birds eat insects AND nest in trees?_____
   _____

✦ On the back of this page write three of your own 'AND' questions about these records.

Searching databases – 3

Learning objectives

- To understand that information can be searched using more than one criterion.
- To search a database using 'OR'.
- To identify the difference between an 'AND' and an 'OR' search.

Resources

- Photocopiable page 66 (optional).
- Data-handling software that uses logical operators including 'AND' and 'OR' for searching data.
- A prepared database, for example insects.

Whole class introduction

- Remind the children about the 'AND' searches they carried out in Lesson 4. Tell them that they will be learning how to carry out a different type of search using the word 'OR'. Use a familiar example first – ask the children to put up their hands or stand up in response to these questions: 'Who has brown hair?', 'Who has blue eyes?', 'Who has a sister?' and so on.
- Then use some 'AND' examples, such as 'Who has blue eyes AND brown hair?' and 'Who has blue eyes AND a sister?'
- Next, introduce the word 'OR', by asking questions such as 'Who has blue eyes OR brown hair?' Make sure they understand that both children with blue eyes and children with brown hair can respond to this question. They need to be aware that 'OR' is used in an inclusive not exclusive sense.
- You may like to use the record cards on page 66 to practise further 'AND' and 'OR' type questions and to emphasise the difference between the two searches. Challenge the children to think up their own 'OR' type questions.

Group activities

Focus group – with the teacher

- Show the children how to carry out an 'OR' search using the prepared database. You may like to tell them to imagine that they are going to develop a wildlife area at school that will have a pond and a garden. They could then search the records by looking at the field habitat and enter 'ponds OR gardens' to see what insects would be likely to inhabit their wildlife area.

Using the photocopiable activity sheets

- Use the activity sheets before the computer session.

Plenary session

Share the responses to the activity sheets – what problems did the children have? Compare this activity with the computer search. Which search is easier to do? Why? Which one do they think is more accurate? Why? What do they have to remember each time they begin a new search? (Make sure they use ALL the records again or else the search will only look at those records from the previous search.)

ICT Skills

◆ Flying insects ◆

✦ Use these records cards to answer the questions below.

name: cranefly	1
max. length: 60mm	
wingspan: 38mm	
colour: brown, black, grey	
habitat: near water	
food (adult): none or nectar	
egg site: soil	
distribution: worldwide	

name: green lacewing	2
max. length: 20mm	
wingspan: 30mm	
colour: green	
habitat: forests, fields, garden, parks	
food (adult): aphids, mites	
egg site: flower stalks	
distribution: worldwide except Australia, New Zealand	

name: housefly	3
max. length: 10mm	
wingspan: 13mm	
colour: grey, black	
habitat: houses, rubbish	
food (adult): human food, rubbish	
egg site: rotten food, rubbish	
distribution: worldwide	

name: emperor dragonfly	4
max. length: 80mm	
wingspan: 105mm	
colour: green-blue, brown	
habitat: near water	
food (adult): flying insects	
egg site: aquatic plants	
distribution: Europe, Mediterranean, Central Asia	

name: mayfly	5
max. length: 12mm	
wingspan: 20mm	
colour: brown, black	
habitat: near water	
food (adult): none	
egg site: rocks in water	
distribution: worldwide	

name: bumble-bee	6
max. length: 27mm	
wingspan: 38mm	
colour: black, yellow	
habitat: gardens, parks	
food (adult): nectar, pollen	
egg site: underground, walls	
distribution: worldwide	

name: potter wasp	7
max. length: 16mm	
wingspan: 20mm	
colour: black and yellow	
habitat: forests, fields, gardens, parks	
food (adult): nectar	
egg site: ground, plants, cells of soil	
distribution: worldwide	

name: hover-fly	8
max. length: 34mm	
wingspan: 25mm	
colour: black, blue, yellow stripes	
habitat: gardens, parks, fields, woods	
food (adult): pollen, nectar	
egg site: plants	
distribution: worldwide	

name: mosquito	9
max. length: 6mm	
wingspan: 9mm	
colour: brown	
habitat: water, animal and human dwellings	
food (adult): males - nectar, females - blood	
egg site: water	
distribution: tropics, Europe	

✦ Tick the correct answer.

1. Name the insects that eat aphids OR eat human food.

    lacewing, housefly ☐

    mosquito, wasp, mayfly ☐

2. Name the insects that lay their eggs on flowers OR in walls.

    cranefly, dragonfly ☐

    lacewing, bumble-bee ☐

3. Name the insects that are black AND live in gardens.

    bumble-bee, wasp, hover-fly ☐

    cranefly, mayfly ☐

4. Name the insects that are black OR live in gardens.

    lacewing, bumble-bee, wasp, hover-fly ☐

    cranefly, lacewing, housefly, mayfly, bumble-bee, wasp, hover-fly ☐

✦ Flying insects ✦

✦ Use these record cards to answer the questions below.

name: cranefly	1
max. length: 60mm	
wingspan: 38mm	
colour: brown, black, grey	
habitat: near water	
food (adult): none or nectar	
egg site: soil	
distribution: worldwide	

name: green lacewing	2
max. length: 20mm	
wingspan: 30mm	
colour: green	
habitat: forests, fields, garden, parks	
food (adult): aphids, mites	
egg site: flower stalks	
distribution: worldwide except Australia, New Zealand	

name: housefly	3
max. length: 10mm	
wingspan: 13mm	
colour: grey, black	
habitat: houses, rubbish	
food (adult): human food, rubbish	
egg site: rotten food, rubbish	
distribution: worldwide	

name: emperor dragonfly	4
max. length: 80mm	
wingspan: 105mm	
colour: green-blue, brown	
habitat: near water	
food (adult): flying insects	
egg site: aquatic plants	
distribution: Europe, Mediterranean, Central Asia	

name: mayfly	5
max. length: 12mm	
wingspan: 20mm	
colour: brown, black	
habitat: near water	
food (adult): none	
egg site: rocks in water	
distribution: worldwide	

name: bumble-bee	6
max. length: 27mm	
wingspan: 38mm	
colour: black, yellow	
habitat: gardens, parks	
food (adult): nectar, pollen	
egg site: underground, walls	
distribution: worldwide	

name: potter wasp	7
max. length: 16mm	
wingspan: 20mm	
colour: black and yellow	
habitat: forests, fields, gardens, parks	
food (adult): nectar	
egg site: ground, plants, cells of soil	
distribution: worldwide	

name: hover-fly	8
max. length: 34mm	
wingspan: 25mm	
colour: black, blue, yellow stripes	
habitat: gardens, parks, fields, woods	
food (adult): pollen, nectar	
egg site: plants	
distribution: worldwide	

name: mosquito	9
max. length: 6mm	
wingspan: 9mm	
colour: brown	
habitat: water, animal and human dwellings	
food (adult): males - nectar, females - blood	
egg site: water	
distribution: tropics, Europe	

1. Name the insects that eat aphids OR eat human food. _____

2. Name the insects that lay their eggs on flowers OR on rubbish. _____

3. Name the insects that have a wing span over 40mm OR a body length over 30mm.

   _____

4. Name the insects that are black AND live in gardens. _____

5. Name the insects that are black OR live in gardens. _____

   _____

6. Write your own OR question using these records.

   _____

✦ Flying insects ✦

✦ Use the records below to answer the questions.

name: cranefly	1
max. length: 60mm	
wingspan: 38mm	
colour: brown, black, grey	
habitat: near water	
food (adult): none or nectar	
egg site: soil	
distribution: worldwide	

name: green lacewing	2
max. length: 20mm	
wingspan: 30mm	
colour: green	
habitat: forests, fields, garden, parks	
food (adult): aphids, mites	
egg site: flower stalks	
distribution: worldwide except Australia, New Zealand	

name: housefly	3
max. length: 10mm	
wingspan: 13mm	
colour: grey, black	
habitat: houses, rubbish	
food (adult): human food, rubbish	
egg site: rotten food, rubbish	
distribution: worldwide	

name: emperor dragonfly	4
max. length: 80mm	
wingspan: 105mm	
colour: green-blue, brown	
habitat: near water	
food (adult): flying insects	
egg site: aquatic plants	
distribution: Europe, Mediterranean, Central Asia	

name: mayfly	5
max. length: 12mm	
wingspan: 20mm	
colour: brown, black	
habitat: near water	
food (adult): none	
egg site: rocks in water	
distribution: worldwide	

name: bumble-bee	6
max. length: 27mm	
wingspan: 38mm	
colour: black, yellow	
habitat: gardens, parks	
food (adult): nectar, pollen	
egg site: underground, walls	
distribution: worldwide	

name: potter wasp	7
max. length: 16mm	
wingspan: 20mm	
colour: black and yellow	
habitat: forests, fields, gardens, parks	
food (adult): nectar	
egg site: ground, plants, cells of soil	
distribution: worldwide	

name: hover-fly	8
max. length: 34mm	
wingspan: 25mm	
colour: black, blue, yellow stripes	
habitat: gardens, parks, fields, woods	
food (adult): pollen, nectar	
egg site: plants	
distribution: worldwide	

name: mosquito	9
max. length: 6mm	
wingspan: 9mm	
colour: brown	
habitat: water, animal and human dwellings	
food (adult): males - nectar, females - blood	
egg site: water	
distribution: tropics, Europe	

1. Name the insects that lay their eggs on plants OR eat rubbish._____

    _____

2. Name the insects that have a wing span of between 20–40mm OR are less than 10mm in

    length. _____

3. Name the insects that are more than 20mm in length AND live in gardens._____

    _____

4. Name the insects that are more than 20mm in length OR live in gardens._____

    _____

5. Write your own OR question using these records.

    _____

Lesson 6

Data accuracy – 1

Learning objectives

✦ To skim-read information to check its relevance and accuracy.
✦ To recognise that information held on IT systems comes from a variety of sources.
✦ To check databases for accuracy and modify a search if necessary.

Resources

✦ Photocopiable page 67.
✦ American CD-Rom encyclopaedia.
✦ Internet access (optional).

Whole class introduction

✦ Photocopy page 67 (enough for each child or pair to have a copy) and cut the page in half, giving the children the top half only. Explain that you want them to find some information about Manchester and that you have run off some copies of information from a website. They will assume you mean Manchester in the UK. Write up the following questions: In what county is Manchester?, On what river does it lie?, What industries does it have?, What colleges are there?, What kinds of museums does it have? and What is its population? Ask the children to skim-read the information to find the answers. Say that they only have a short time to do this and that the class will come together again in a few minutes. (Some children might realise straight away that the information is actually about Manchester in the USA. Quietly ask them to find the answers about this city anyway while the others work on.)
✦ When did the children realise that they were looking at a website for the wrong Manchester? What do they think went wrong? Why wasn't this information relevant to Manchester in the UK? What clues in the text first alerted them to this fact? What clues tell them that the website is American (such as 'center')?
✦ How would we have to change our search on the Internet (or CD-Rom encyclopaedia) to make sure we find information about Manchester, England?

Discuss different types of searches (for example Manchester AND England; Manchester, England; Manchester + England; Manchester AND NOT USA) and explain that different CD-Roms and Internet search engines use different methods.

✦ Discuss the accuracy of websites and how they can be produced. Tell them that anyone can put a website together and that the information they include is not necessarily correct or relevant. They need to keep this in mind when carrying out searches. How can they tell how up-to-date the information on the Manchester USA website is? What can we do to make sure they are not getting incorrect/irrelevant information? (Carry out several searches in more than one site to collate findings, use recommended sites, check when the site was last updated and so on.)
✦ Hand out the second half of page 67 and ask the children to skim-read this to find the answers to the original questions.

Group activities

Focus group – with the teacher

✦ Explain that, like the Internet, CD-Rom encyclopaedias can contain information that may not be relevant for their purpose. Use an American CD-Rom encyclopaedia and ask the children to find information about topics such as Portsmouth, Newport, football and London. How do they have to modify their searches to locate English information?

Using the photocopiable activity sheets

✦ Use the sheets before or after the computer session.

Plenary session

Share the responses to the activity sheets. What do they need to be aware of when finding information? (Relevancy, accuracy.) How can we ensure that the information we find is as accurate as possible?

✦ Plymouth ✦

✦ Skim-read these three text extracts to answer the questions below.

Plymouth, a city in Devon, England, lies on Plymouth Sound and the Plym and Tamar rivers. It has a very good natural harbor and is the site of the Royal Naval Dockyard. It is also a major fishing port. Plymouth has a new aquarium (1998), a zoo, several museums and a college. Population (1991) 238 800. maintained by <u>Plymouth Tourism</u>, last update Jan 2000	Of all the old ports of England with their great history, only Plymouth is still of real importance today. All of the other small ports, such as Dartmouth, were bombed – indeed the famous Butterwalk is only just standing. But Plymouth is one of the most heavily damaged and much building work is needed to restore it to its former glory.	Plymouth is a town situated on Plymouth Bay about 55km southeast of Boston, USA. It was the site of the first permanent European settlement in New England and is now a fishing and tourist center. Among the many attractions are Plymouth Rock, Burial Hill cemetery and the Mayflower II. Population (1990) 45 608 *home* *index*
A	**B**	**C**

1. Circle the correct answer.

    a   Which extract do you think is very out-of-date?   **A**   **B**   **C**

    b   Which extract(s) do you think is/are from an American source?

         A   **B**   **C**

    c   Which extract(s) tell you about Plymouth, England?

         A   **B**   **C**

    d   Which extract(s) would NOT help you find out about Plymouth, USA?

         A   **B**   **C**

    e   Which extracts would you read to compare the population of Plymouth, England with Plymouth in the USA?

         A   **B**   **C**

2. On which rivers does Plymouth, England lie?_____

3. Name two tourist attractions in Plymouth, USA. _____

✦ Plymouth ✦

✦ Skim-read these three text extracts to answer the questions below.

A	B	C
Plymouth, a city in Devon, lies on Plymouth Sound and the Plym and Tamar rivers. It has a very good natural harbor and is the site of the Royal Naval Dockyard. It is also a major fishing port. Plymouth has a new aquarium (1998), a zoo, several museums and a college. Population (1991) 238 800. maintained by Plymouth Tourism, last update Jan 2000	Of all the old ports of England with their great history only Plymouth is still of real importance today. All of the other small ports such as Dartmouth were bombed - indeed the famous Butter-walk is only just standing. But Plymouth is one of the most heavily damaged and much building work is needed to restore it to its former glory.	Plymouth is a town situated on Plymouth Bay about 55km southeast of Boston. It was the site of the first permanent European settlement in New England and is now a fishing and tourist center. Among the many attractions are Plymouth Rock, Burial Hill cemetery and the Mayflower II. Population (1990) 45 608 *home* *index*

1. Which extract(s) do you think is/are very out-of-date? Why?_____

    _____

2. Which extract(s) do you think is/are from American sources? Say why you think this.

    _____

3. Which extract(s) is/are about Plymouth, England?_____

4. Which extract(s) would NOT help you find out about Plymouth, USA?_____

5. Which extracts would you read to compare the population of Plymouth, England with that

    of Plymouth, USA?_____

6. What section of extract C would you use to find out about cinemas in Plymouth?

    _____

7. On which rivers does Plymouth, England lie? _____

8. Name two tourist attractions in Plymouth, USA._____

9. Name two tourist attractions in Plymouth, England._____

10. When was the new aquarium opened in Plymouth, England?_____

✦ Plymouth ✦

✦ Skim read these three text extracts to answer the questions below.

A

Plymouth, a city in Devon, lies on Plymouth Sound and the Plym and Tamar rivers. It has a very good natural harbor and is the site of the Royal Naval Dockyard. It is also a major fishing port.

Plymouth has a new aquarium (1998), a zoo, several museums and a college.
Population (1991) 238 800.

maintained by Plymouth Tourism, last update Jan 2000

B

Of all the old ports of England with their great history only Plymouth is still of real importance today. All of the other small ports such as Dartmouth were bombed - indeed the famous Butter-walk is only just standing. But Plymouth is one of the most heavily damaged and much building work is needed to restore it to its former glory.

C

Plymouth is a town situated on Plymouth Bay about 55km southeast of Boston. It was the site of the first permanent European settlement in New England and is now a fishing and tourist center.

Among the many attractions are Plymouth Rock, Burial Hill cemetery and the Mayflower II.
Population (1990) 45 608

home   *index*

1. Which extract(s) do you think is/are very out-of-date? Why?_____

_____

2. Which extract(s) do you think is/are from American sources? Say why you think this.

_____

3. Which extract(s) is/are about Plymouth, England?_____

4. Which extract(s) would NOT help you find out about Plymouth, USA?_____

5. Who could you contact to find out more about Plymouth, England?_____

_____

6. Which extract suggests that we can find out more about Plymouth? What tells you this?

_____

7. Why do you think the population figure for Plymouth, England is for 1991 and yet the

information was last updated in January 2000?_____

_____

8. What things does Plymouth, England have in common with Plymouth, USA?_____

_____

Data accuracy – 2

 Learning objectives

◆ To understand that information sources can contain errors and inaccuracies.
◆ To identify some of the implications of incorrect data.
◆ To understand that if databases contain errors this can affect results of searches.
◆ To check a database for accuracy by checking data.

 Resources

◆ Photocopiable page 68.
◆ Data-handling software.
◆ Prepared data files containing errors.

 Whole class introduction

◆ Ask the children to remind you what a database is. What kinds of databases might be used every day? Discuss different types, such as the pupil database at school, databases collected by supermarket loyalty cards, bank databases, Internet sites and so on. Why are these databases necessary? What could people use the databases for? (For example, supermarkets might send their customers advertising leaflets and banks might send customers statements.)
◆ Ask the children to tell you how they think the information for the databases is gathered/collected. What might happen if the information gathered is incorrect? What might happen if the person inputting the information into a computer makes a mistake? How might this affect the customer? Discuss the World Wide Web – will all the information in all sites be accurate/correct? Why/why not?
◆ Show the children an enlarged version of page 68 (or provide each pair with their own copy). Explain that a clothing company called *Teen-Scene Clothing* wanted to carry out a survey to find out about the measurements and favourite colours of children aged between 13 and 16 and these are the results. Tell them that there were several errors in the compilation of the data and

ask them to read through the information to see if they can spot them. (There are only two boys, therefore the survey is biased towards girls; an incorrect field type is given – girl instead of female; there are incorrect measurements on several records and one person was over the age of 16.)
◆ Discuss how the errors may have come about when the questionnaire was completed. Has the survey been worthwhile for the company? What would they need to do to redress this?
◆ Explain that they are now going to check for errors in both a recorded-onto-paper database and a computer-based database.

 Group activities

Focus group – with the teacher

◆ Ask the children to check through the prepared database that contains errors. Ask them to write down what the errors are and how they might affect the results.

Using the photocopiable activity sheets

◆ The activity sheets could be used before or after the computer session.

 Plenary session

Share the responses to the activity sheets and the computer session. Did the children find all the errors? How important would it be to correct each of these errors? What would you do if you could not confirm one record's information? (It may be better to delete one record than have this record corrupt the whole database.) How important is it to check the source of the data before it is changed? (The person's own knowledge of the data may be limited and therefore they may inadvertently change something that they thought was incorrect but was in fact correct.)

◆ Spot the mistakes! ◆

◆ Read through these questionnaires completed in January 2000 by people aged from 13 to 16 for *Teen-Scene Clothing* company. There is a mistake in each one. Write the name of the person whose record has the mistake that is listed. The first one has been done for you.

Name: Andy Waite
DOB: 5. 4. 85
Male/female: male
Height: 165cm
Chest: 8.9cm
Waist: 70cm
Favourite colour: blue

Name: Linda Paul
DOB: 6. 10. 87
Male/female: female
Height: 168cm
Chest: 85cm
Waist: 65cm
Favourite colour: blew

Name: Giles Bagpipe
DOB: 8. 8. 86
Male/female: boy
Height: 170cm
Chest: 92cm
Waist: 75cm
Favourite colour: red

Name: Jodie Watson
DOB: 12. 12. 85
Male/female: female
Height: 168cm
Chest: 89cm
Waist: 720cm
Favourite colour: blue

Name: Ann West
DOB: 25. 7. 86
Male/female: male
Height: 165cm
Chest: 89cm
Waist: 72cm
Favourite colour: green

Name: Ranjit Malane
DOB: 15. 9. 87
Male/female: male
Height: 15.6cm
Chest: 84cm
Waist: 69cm
Favourite colour: brown

Name: Melanie Sweet
DOB: 15. 1. 80
Male/female: female
Height: 172cm
Chest: 95cm
Waist: 76cm
Favourite colour: red

Name: Jason Thames
DOB: 28. 14. 85
Male/female: male
Height: 156cm
Chest: 87cm
Waist: 67cm
Favourite colour: blue

Mistakes:

1. person is too old for 13 to 16 age group: <u>Melanie Sweet</u>

2. waist measurement must be wrong _____

3. date of birth is incorrect _____

4. chest measurement must be wrong _____

5. listed as male but this person is female _____

6. spelling of favourite colour is incorrect _____

7. the word 'boy' is used instead of 'male' _____

8. height measurement must be wrong _____

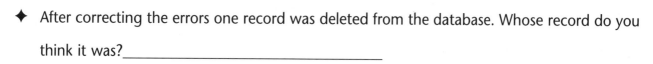

◆ After correcting the errors one record was deleted from the database. Whose record do you

think it was?_____

Why?_____

✦ Spot the mistakes! ✦

✦ Read through these questionnaires completed in January 2000 by people aged from 13 to 16 for *Teen-Scene Clothing* company. You will find one error in each record. Write the mistake underneath each one. The first one has been done for you.

Name: Andy Waite
DOB: 5. 4. 85
Male/female: male
Height: 165cm
Chest: 8.9cm
Waist: 70cm
Favourite colour: blue

error:

chest measurement
must be incorrect

Name: Linda Paul
DOB: 6. 10. 87
Male/female: female
Height: 168cm
Chest: 85cm
Waist: 65cm
Favourite colour: blew

error:

_____
_____

Name: Giles Bagpipe
DOB: 8. 8. 86
Male/female: boy
Height: 170cm
Chest: 92cm
Waist: 75cm
Favourite colour: red

error:

_____
_____

Name: Jodie Watson
DOB: 12. 12. 85
Male/female: female
Height: 168cm
Chest: 89cm
Waist: 720cm
Favourite colour: blue

error:

_____
_____

Name: Ann West
DOB: 25. 7. 86
Male/female: male
Height: 165cm
Chest: 89cm
Waist: 72cm
Favourite colour: green

error:

_____
_____

Name: Ranjit Malane
DOB: 15. 9. 87
Male/female: male
Height: 15.6cm
Chest: 84cm
Waist: 69cm
Favourite colour: brown

error:

_____
_____

Name: Melanie Sweet
DOB: 15. 1. 80
Male/female: female
Height: 172cm
Chest: 95cm
Waist: 76cm
Favourite colour: red

error:

_____
_____

Name: Jason Thames
DOB: 28. 14. 85
Male/female: male
Height: 156cm
Chest: 87cm
Waist: 67cm
Favourite colour: blue

error:

_____
_____

✦ Now answer these questions.

1. Which person's record would you delete from the survey?_____

   Why?_____

2. What colour should *Teen-Scene Clothing* use in their new clothes?_____

   Why?_____

ICT Skills

✦ Spot the mistakes! ✦

✦ Read through these questionnaires completed in January 2000 by people aged from 13 to 16 for *Teen-Scene Clothing* company. Find the mistakes.

Name: Andy Waite **DOB:** 5. 4. 85 **Male/female:** male **Height:** 165cm **Chest:** 8.9cm **Waist:** 70cm **Favourite colour:** blue	**Name:** Linda Paul **DOB:** 6. 10. 87 **Male/female:** female **Height:** 168cm **Chest:** 85cm **Waist:** 65cm **Favourite colour:** blew	**Name:** Giles Bagpipe **DOB:** 8. 8. 86 **Male/female:** boy **Height:** 170cm **Chest:** 92cm **Waist:** seventy-five cm **Favourite colour:** red	**Name:** Jodie Watson **DOB:** 12. 12. 85 **Male/female:** female **Height:** 168cm **Chest:** 89cm **Waist:** 720cm **Favourite colour:** blue
Name: Ann West **DOB:** 25. 7. 86 **Male/female:** male **Height:** 165cm **Chest:** 890cm **Waist:** 72cm **Favourite colour:** green	**Name:** Ranjit Malane **DOB:** 15. 9. 87 **Male/female:** male **Height:** 15.6cm **Chest:** 84cm **Waist:** 69cm **Favourite colour:** brown	**Name:** Melanie Sweet **DOB:** 15. 1. 80 **Male/female:** female **Height:** 172cm **Chest:** 95cm **Waist:** 76cm **Favourite colour:** redd	**Name:** Jason Thames **DOB:** 28. 14. 85 **Male/female:** male **Height:** 156cm **Chest:** 87cm **Waist:** 67cm **Favourite colour:** blue

✦ Write your list of mistakes here.

✦ Now answer these questions.

1. Which person's record would you delete from the survey?_____

   Why?_____

2. What colour should *Teen-Scene Clothing* use in their new clothes?_____

   Why?_____

3. Do you consider this to be a fair survey? Why or why not?_____

   _____

Lesson 8

Data accuracy – 3

Learning objectives

✦ To understand that line graphs may contain errors which affect interpretation.
✦ To check for anomalies in graphical representations.
✦ To identify and correct inaccurate data when using ICT.

Resources

✦ Photocopiable pages 68 and 69.
✦ Data-handling software.
✦ Prepared data file containing continuous data (for example temperature) that contains one error.

Whole class introduction

✦ Enlarge page 69 on the photocopier. Cut out the four separate graphs and charts.
✦ Show the children page 68 and remind them about the errors they found in the questionnaire survey for *Teen-Scene Clothing* in Lesson 7. Tell them they are going to consider some more things about the information in this survey.
✦ Explain that the clothing company wants to find out the average height of the children in the survey so they can decide how long to make their clothing. Ask the children to remind you how to find the average. Share the chart of height measurements from page 69. Tell them the shortest, tallest and average height measurements and ask them to consider if they think the average height seems correct.
✦ Discuss the following points:
  – the incorrect height for Julia may not be very noticeable when in chart form but when entered into a database and an average found or a graph produced (show the bar line graph) the error becomes very obvious.
  – how would this affect the clothing company? (The average height is actually 164cm; therefore all their clothing would be too short if based on 156cm.) One error can therefore skew the results.
✦ Share the temperature example on page 69. What do they notice about this graph? Which part do

they think is incorrect? Why? Explain that if a person was entering lots of temperatures into a database, the incorrect one for 14.00 might not be noticed, but when a line graph is produced, it becomes very obvious that something is wrong, as it would be highly unlikely for the temperature to drop so low in an hour and then rise rapidly again.
✦ Tell the children that they should always check carefully when gathering, recording and entering data but they should also try to develop the confidence to question any information produced from the database that they think might be inaccurate. Remind them that the information contained in a computer relies on the accuracy of the person who gathered and entered it.

Group activities

Focus group – with the teacher

✦ Use the prepared data file and ask the children to find the one error contained in it. They could make a prediction first by checking through the records and then test their prediction by producing a line graph.

Using the photocopiable activity sheets

✦ The sheets could be used before or after the computer session. Answers – page 62.

Plenary session

Share the answers to the activity sheets. Did everyone spot all the mistakes? How would this affect the results? Share the line graphs produced on the computer. Were the children's predictions correct? How effective are the graphs in highlighting mistakes?

◆ Spot the mistakes 2 ◆

◆ Spot the mistakes in these charts and graphs. Put a circle around the information that you think is incorrect.

1

Bus timetable – Friday

Departure	Arrival
09.00	09.30
09.30	10.00
10.00	10.30
10.30	11.00
11.00	11.30
11.03	12.00
12.00	12.30
12.30	13.00
13.00	13.30

2

Hourly Temperatures – Monday

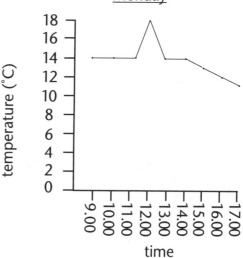

3

Types of homes we live in

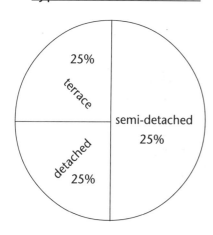

◆ On the back of this page draw your own graph or chart and include one error in it. Show it to a friend. Can they find the mistake?

4

Our heights

Name		Height
1	Maria	150cm
2	Jason	158cm
3	Ellie	155cm
4	Ahmed	158cm
5	Anne	157cm
6	Sara	156cm
7	Chris	158cm
8	Jeannie	154cm
9	Maya	154cm
10	Tanya	158cm
11	Lucy	150mm
12	Karen	152cm
13	Angel	155cm
14	Michael	152cm
15	Laurie	151cm
16	John	150cm

✦ Spot the mistakes 2 ✦

✦ Spot the mistakes in these charts and graphs. Put a circle around the information that you think is incorrect. Correct the mistake by writing in what you think it should be.

1

Bus timetable – Friday

Departure	Arrival
09.00	09.45
09.50	10.35
10.40	11.25
11.30	12.05
12.20	13.05
13.10	13.55
14.00	14.45
14.50	15.35
15.40	16.25

2

Hourly Temperatures – Monday

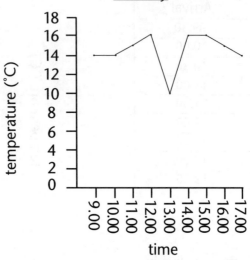

3

Types of homes we live in

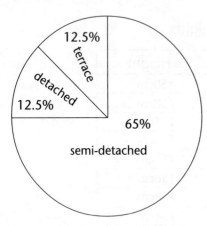

4

Our heights

	Name	Height
1	Maria	1.50m
2	Jason	1.58m
3	Ellie	1.55m
4	Ahmed	1.58m
5	Anne	1.57m
6	Sara	156m
7	Chris	1.58m
8	Jeannie	1.54m
9	Maya	1.54m
10	Tanya	1.58m
11	Lucy	1.50m
12	Karen	1.52m
13	Angel	1.55m
14	Michael	1.52m
15	Laurie	1.51m
16	John	1.50m

✦ On the back of this page draw your own graph or chart and include one error in it. Show it to a friend. Can they find the mistake?

✦ Spot the mistakes 2 ✦

✦ Spot the mistakes in these charts and graphs. Put a circle around the information that you think is incorrect. Correct the mistake by writing in what you think it should be.

1

Bus timetable – Friday

Departure	Arrival
09.00	10.35
10.50	12.25
12.40	14.15
14.30	16.05
16.20	17.45
18.10	19.45
20.00	21.35
21.50	23.25
23.40	01.15

2

Hourly Temperatures – Monday and Tuesday

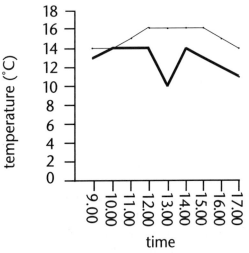

Mon = ——
Tues = ▬▬

Av. temp:
Mon = 15.1
Tues = 13.2

3

Types of homes we live in

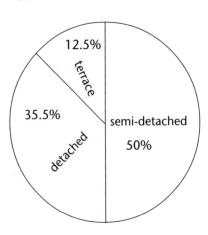

12.5% terrace
35.5% detached
semi-detached 50%

4

Our heights

Name		Height
1	Maria	1.50m
2	Jason	1.58m
3	Ellie	1.55m
4	Ahmed	1.58m
5	Anne	1.57m
6	Sara	156 m
7	Chris	1.58m
8	Jeannie	1.54m
9	Maya	1.54m
10	Tanya	1.58m
11	Lucy	1.50m
12	Karen	1.52m
13	Angel	1.55m
14	Michael	1.52m
15	Laurie	1.51m
16	John	1.50m

Av. height:

11.20m

✦ On the back of this page draw your own graph or chart and include one error in it. Show it to a friend. Can they find the mistake?

Lesson 9

Spreadsheets – introduction

 Learning objectives

✦ To understand how a spreadsheet can be used to carry out calculations.
✦ To understand that costing models may need to be changed.
✦ To enter labels and numbers into a spreadsheet.
✦ To know that computers can calculate costs.

 Resources

✦ Photocopiable page 70.
✦ Spreadsheet software.
✦ Calculators.

 Whole class introduction

✦ Enlarge page 70 on a photocopier or copy it out onto the board. Tell the children that they are going to help you plan a holiday to the Algarve! Explain that you have a budget of £750.00 and that you would like them to help you use a spreadsheet to work out the total cost of the holiday.
✦ Explain what a spreadsheet is by using page 70 as an example. Ask the children to tell you the costs of the flight, taxi, villa and insurance by referring to the holiday information shown on the sheet. Show them how to enter this data correctly on the spreadsheet. Use technical terms such as column, row and cell as you enter the data. Ask questions such as 'In which cell will I enter the cost of the insurance?' (B8), or 'What amount will I enter into cell B3? (£149.00) Ask someone to add up the total so far, using a calculator. Agree on the amount you will budget for food and spending money. Recalculate the total. Agree the heading for column B (for example, 1 adult).
✦ Now explain that, having made your plans, you went in to book your holiday only to discover that the flight costs have increased to £189.00. How will this affect your budget? Redo the costings by crossing out and changing the amount in B3, keeping the taxi, villa and insurance the same. How will this now affect the food and spending

money – what adjustments need to be made to these cells to stay within the £750.00 budget?
✦ Ask the children to use the information on page 70 to complete other budgeting possibilities in the spreadsheet, such as two adults or a family going on the same holiday (decide on their budget). What costs will remain the same? What costs will change? Keep reminding the children of the correct technical terms of row, column and cell as you enter the new data.

 Group activities

Focus group – with the teacher

✦ Set up a spreadsheet on the computer to match the example on page 70. Tell the children that a computer can be used to produce a spreadsheet in exactly the same way as they did in the class lesson. Show them how to move around the spreadsheet and how to enter numbers and labels. Ask the children to produce a table using the earlier information about the holiday costs. Ask them to change the amounts in some of the cells (as was modelled in the class introduction).
✦ Show them how the computer can add the total amount for a column and tell them that they will be learning how to do this themselves in their next lesson.

Using the photocopiable activity sheets

✦ The sheets should be used before the computer session.

 Plenary session

Share the responses to the activity sheets. What problems did they have? Compare entering and changing data on the activity sheet with the computer. Which one is easier? Which one gives us a neater presentation? What other uses can the children suggest for a spreadsheet?

✦ Holiday budgeting ✦

✦ Complete the spreadsheet below for a 1 week holiday for 1 adult by using the available information. Use a calculator to find the total.

	A	B
1	*item*	*1 adult*
2	taxi to airport	
3	flight	
4	villa	
5	food	
6	spending money	
7	taxi home	
8	insurance	
9	*total*	

flight – **(B3)**
£150.00 each person over 2 years of age

taxi to airport – **(B2 and B7)**
£25.00 each way

villa (per week) – **(B4)**
up to 2 adults – £250.00
family – £400.00

holiday insurance

insurance (up to 7 days): (B8)
1 adult – £14.50
family – £30.00

insurance (up to 14 days):
1 adult – £18.50
family – £40.00

food – **(B5)**
£100.00

spending money – **(B6)**
£200.00

◆ Holiday budgeting ◆

✦ Use the holiday information below to complete the spreadsheet in the following way:

Column B – 1 week holiday for 1 adult (budget – £760)

Column C – 1 week holiday for 2 adults (budget – £1000.00)

Use a calculator to help you.

	A	B	C
1	*item*	*1 adult*	*2 adults*
2	taxi to airport		
3	flight		
4	villa		
5	food		
6	spending money		
7	taxi home		
8	insurance		
9	*total*		

flight
£142.00 each person
over 2 years of age

holiday insurance

insurance (up to 7 days):
1 adult – £14.99
family – £29.99

insurance (up to 14 days):
1 adult – £18.99
family – £39.99

taxi to airport
£25.00 each way

villa (per week)
up to 2 adults – £250.00
family – £400.00

✦ Holiday budgeting ✦

✦ Use the holiday information below to complete the spreadsheet in the following way:

Column B – 1 week holiday for 1 adult (budget – £760)

Column C – 2 week holiday for 2 adults and two children aged 10 and 12 (budget – £2100.00)

Use a calculator to help you.

	A	B	C
1	*item*	*1 adult*	*family*
2	taxi to airport		
3	flight		
4	villa		
5	food		
6	spending money		
7	taxi home		
8	insurance		
9	*total*		

<u>holiday insurance</u>

insurance (up to 7 days):
1 adult – £14.99
family – £29.99

insurance (up to 14 days):
1 adult – £18.99
family – £39.99

<u>flight</u>
£142.00 each person over 2 years of age

taxi to airport
£25.00 each way

<u>villa (per week)</u>
up to 2 adults – £250.00
family – £400.00

✦ Now work out the budgets for the same two holidays but with a flight increase of £16.00 per person. Make your alterations in red.

Lesson 10

Spreadsheets – using formulae

 Learning objectives

- ✦ To understand how to use simple formulae.
- ✦ To enter data and formulae into a spreadsheet.
- ✦ To modify data in a spreadsheet, make predictions of changes and check results.

 Resources

- ✦ Photocopiable page 70.
- ✦ Spreadsheet software.
- ✦ Calculators.

 Whole class introduction

- ✦ Remind the children about the spreadsheet activities they carried out in Lesson 9. Explain that they will now be learning how to use formulae to calculate sums on the spreadsheet.
- ✦ If necessary, explain what a formula is. (A rule which contains an equals sign. A rule written as an equation – where both sides of the equals sign balance each other.) Explore several examples, such as: $a + 4 = 10$, area = $l \times b$, to ensure the children understand what a formula is.
- ✦ Use page 70 as a basis for exploring formulae further. For example, introduce the idea of spreadsheet formulae, such as: B9 = B2 + B3 + B4 + B5 + B6 + B7 + B8. Explain that if we added another row to each column (to make B10, C10, D10 and E10) we could do other calculations, such as: B10 = B9 – B8 to find out how much the holiday would cost without insurance. Use a calculator to find the answers but explain that you will be showing them how the computer can do these calculations for them.
- ✦ Ask the children to complete the activity sheets before using the computer to ensure they understand how to use simple formulae.

 Group activities

Focus group – with the teacher

- ✦ Enter two numbers into two cells (for example, A1 and A2). Show the children how to enter a formula into the formula bar to calculate the sum of A1 and A2 and have the answer appear in A4. (Do this by highlighting A4 then typing '= A1 + A2' and press enter. A4 will then show the answer to the sum. Note: you must include the = sign before the rest of the formula.) Ask the children to explore what happens when the data in the two cells is changed. (The sum in A4 automatically changes.) Then ask them to enter a longer column of numbers and change the formula to calculate the sum.
- ✦ Next ask the children to explore subtraction, multiplication and division formulae. Ask them to change the data in a cell and predict what the change will do to the total. Then ask them to check the result.

Using the photocopiable activity sheets

- ✦ The activity sheets should be completed before the computer session.

 Plenary session

Share the responses to the activity sheets. Did the children find the formulae easy to follow? Compare the manual adding for the activity sheets with the computer spreadsheet. Discuss ease of use, time taken and accuracy. If some data had to be changed which method would do this more easily – computer or calculator? What uses can the children suggest for a spreadsheet – at home? at school? in offices? How might it help them?

✦ Holiday spending ✦

✦ The Elvin family have just been on holiday. This chart shows what they spent their money on.

	A	B	C	D
1	item	Jenny	Barry	Maddy
2	magazines/books	11.25	6.99	6.00
3	clothes	25.00	0.00	50.00
4	ice-creams	6.93	4.95	13.86
5	souvenirs	5.00	5.00	12.00
6	total			

✦ Work out these calculations. Write the answers in the empty boxes. Use a calculator to help you.

1. How much Jenny spent altogether.

   (B6 =B2 + B3 + B4 + B5)

2. How much Maddy spent altogether.

   (D6 =D2 + D3 + D4 + D5)

3. How much Barry spent altogether.

   (C6 = C2 + C3 + C4 + C5)

	B
1	Jenny
2	11.25
3	25.00
4	6.93
5	5.00
6	

	D
1	Maddy
2	6.00
3	50.00
4	13.86
5	12.00
6	

	C
1	Barry
2	6.99
3	0.00
4	4.95
5	5.00
6	

4. If Maddy only spent £25.00 on clothes instead of £50.00, what would D6 change to?_____

5. If Barry spent £10.00 instead of £5.00 on souvenirs, what would C6 change to?_____

✦ Holiday spending ✦

✦ The Elvin family have just been on holiday. Use the chart below to answer the questions about how much they spent.

	A	B	C	D
1	item	Jenny	Barry	Maddy
2	magazines/books	11.25	6.99	6.00
3	clothes	25.00	0.00	50.00
4	ice-creams	6.93	4.95	13.86
5	souvenirs	5.00	5.00	12.00
6	total			

✦ Use the formula in each question to calculate the sums.
Use a calculator to help you.

1. Find the total of Jenny's spending. B6 = B2 + B3 + B4 + B5

   _____

2. Calculate C6 = C2 + C3 + C4 + C5 _____

3. Find the total of Maddy's spending. D6 = D2 + D3 + D4 + D5.

   _____

4. Calculate how much Jenny spent altogether if she doubled her spending on clothing. (Remember to alter the amount in B3.)
   B6 = B2 + B3 + B4 + B5 _____

5. How much more did Maddy spend on clothes than on ice-creams?
   D6 = D3 – D4 _____

6. How much did Barry spend on magazines and souvenirs?
   C6 = C2 + C5 _____

7. How much less did Jenny spend on souvenirs than on clothes?
   B6 = B3 – B5 _____

8. How much did Maddy spend on clothes and souvenirs?
   D6 = D3 + D5 _____

ICT Skills

✦ Holiday spending ✦

✦ The Elvin family have just been on holiday. Use the chart below to answer the questions about how much they spent.

	A	B	C	D
1	item	Jenny	Barry	Maddy
2	magazines/books	11.25	6.99	6.00
3	clothes	25.00	0.00	50.00
4	ice-creams	6.93	4.95	13.86
5	souvenirs	5.00	5.00	12.00
6	total			

✦ For each question below write the formula and the answer. Use a calculator to help you. The first one has been done for you.

1. Find the total of Jenny's spending.

   Formula: B6 = B2 + B3 + B4 + B5   Answer: £48.18

2. Calculate how much Maddy spent altogether.

   Formula:_____   Answer:_____

3. How much did Barry spend altogether?

   Formula:_____   Answer:_____

4. How much more did Maddy spend on clothes than on ice-creams?

   Formula:_____   Answer:_____

5. Calculate how much Jenny spent altogether if she doubled her spending on clothing.

   Formula: _____   Answer:_____

6. How much would Barry spend if he spent twice his total?

   Formula: _____   Answer:_____

7. How much less did Jenny spend on souvenirs than on clothes?

   Formula: _____   Answer:_____

8. How much would Jenny spend if she spent half her total?

   Formula: _____   Answer:_____

Lesson 11

Spreadsheet calculations

 Learning objectives

✦ To use a spreadsheet to carry out calculations.
✦ To use 'SUM' to calculate the total of a set of numbers in a range of cells.

 Resources

✦ Photocopiable page 71.
✦ Spreadsheet software.
✦ Calculators.

 Whole class introduction

✦ Ask the children to remind you of the work they did with spreadsheets in Lesson 10. Tell them that they will be learning more about spreadsheets today.
✦ Enlarge page 71 on a photocopier or provide each child or pair with their own copy. Explain that the Elvin family went to Aeropark for their holiday and there they saw listed on a display board the daily numbers of visitors to the park for the previous week. Why do the children think the managers of the park might want to know this information? Why might they display it for visitors to see?
✦ Revise the work carried out in Lesson 10 by doing questions 1 to 3 together. Remind them that the answer in cells can change according to the calculation (for example C9 in questions 2 and 3). Then ask the children to consider question 4. How is this different from earlier questions? (They are adding along a row rather than down a column.)
✦ Complete the questions together and then ask the children to suggest the formulae for further questions, such as total number of people for Tuesday (D3 = B3 + C3).

 Group activities

Focus group – with the teacher

✦ Remind the children how, for example, '= B1 + B2 + B3 + B4 + B5' produces a total. Tell them that you are now going to show them a quicker and easier way of producing a total on the spreadsheet. Introduce the use of 'SUM', =SUM(A1:A5), as a shorter way of producing a total. The children could enter the same information as on page 71 to practise entering data and calculating using 'SUM'. Stress the importance of the brackets and make sure the children total both columns and rows in their calculations.

Using the photocopiable activity sheets

✦ The sheets should be used before the computer session.

 Plenary session

Share the responses to the activity sheets. Compare this manual task using a calculator with the computer spreadsheet. Which is easier? Which is more accurate? Which one provides us with better presentation if calculations change? Discuss the ease of using the calculation 'SUM' – does this make the calculations quicker? Why would it be important for a restaurant to do such calculations?

ICT Skills

✦ Airport restaurant ✦

✦ The airport restaurant needs to calculate how many salads were sold in the week and how much it cost them. Help them do this by answering the questions.

	A	B	C	D
	day	no. of salads	unit cost £	total £
1				
2	Monday	980	0.95	931.00
3	Tuesday	1010	0.95	959.50
4	Wednesday	825	0.95	783.75
5	Thursday	460	0.95	
6	Friday	1560	0.95	
7	Saturday	2470	0.95	2346.50
8	Sunday	2450	0.95	
9				
10				

✦ Calculate the following by using the given formulae. Write the answers in the correct cells. Use a calculator to help you.

1. The total number of salads sold in the week. B9 = B2 + B3 + B4 + B5 + B6 + B7 + B8

2. The cost of making the salads for Thursday. D5 = B5 x C5

3. The cost of making the salads for Friday. D6 = B6 x C6

4. The cost of making the salads for Sunday. D8 = B8 x C8

5. The total cost for making the week's salads. D9 = D2 + D3 + D4 + D5 + D6 + D7 + D8

6. The difference between the highest number of salads sold (Saturday) and the lowest (Thursday). B10 = B7 – B5

7. The difference in cost between the highest number sold and the lowest. D10 = D7 – D5

✦ Airport restaurant ✦

✦ The airport restaurant needs to calculate how many salads were sold in the week and how much it cost them. Help them do this by answering the questions.

	A	B	C	D
1	*day*	*no. of salads*	*unit cost £*	*total £*
2	Monday	980	0.95	931.00
3	Tuesday	1010	0.95	
4	Wednesday	825	0.95	
5	Thursday	460	0.95	
6	Friday	1560	0.95	
7	Saturday	2470	0.95	
8	Sunday	2450	0.95	
9				
10				

✦ Calculate the following by using the given formulae. Write the answers in the correct cells. Use a calculator to help you.

1. The total number of salads sold in the week. B9 = B2 + B3 + B4 + B5 + B6 + B7 + B8

2. The cost of making the salads for: **a)** Tuesday (D3 = B3 x C3)

   b) Wednesday (D4 = B4 x C4)   **c)** Thursday (D5 = B5 x C5)

   d) Friday (D6 = B6 x C6)   **e)** Saturday (D7 = B7 x C7)   **f)** Sunday (D8 = B8 x C8)

3. The total cost for making the week's salads. D9 = D2 + D3 + D4 + D5 + D6 + D7 + D8

4. The difference between the highest number of salads sold (Saturday) and the lowest (Thursday). B10 = B7 – B5

5. The difference in cost between the highest number sold and the lowest.
   D10 = D7 – D5

Photocopiable
©Hopscotch Educational Publishing

◆ Airport restaurant ◆

✦ The airport restaurant needs to calculate how many salads were sold in the week and how much it cost them. Help them do this by answering the questions.

	A	B	C	D
1	day	no. of salads	unit cost £	total £
2	Monday	980	0.95	
3	Tuesday	1010	0.95	
4	Wednesday	825	0.95	
5	Thursday	460	0.95	
6	Friday	1560	0.95	
7	Saturday	2470	0.95	
8	Sunday	2450	0.95	
9				
10				

✦ Calculate the following. Write the formula you will use next to each question and the answers in the correct cells. Use a calculator to help you.

1. The total number of salads sold in the week. Formula: _____

2. The cost of making the salads for each day of the week:

   a) Monday – formula:_____   b) Tuesday – formula:_____

   c) Wednesday – formula:_____   d) Thursday – formula:_____

   e) Friday – formula:_____   f) Saturday – formula:_____

   g) Sunday – formula:_____

3. The total cost for making the week's salads. Formula:_____

4. The difference between the highest number of salads sold and the lowest.
   Formula:_____
   The difference in cost between the two days. Formula:_____

Lesson 12

Controlling devices – 1

 Learning objectives

✦ To understand that devices can be controlled through direct instructions.
✦ To know that a control box and software can be used to control an output device.
✦ To control a simple device, such as a light bulb, by giving direct instructions.
✦ To give a sensible estimate and then check by counting.

 Resources

✦ Control box and software that sends instructions from the computer to the control box.
✦ Bulb holders, small bulbs, insulated wire.
✦ Jack plugs which fit the sockets on control box.

Whole class introduction

✦ Begin with a discussion about everyday devices that rely on monitoring and control. For example, an outdoor light that comes on when someone walks in front of it, street lights that come on when it gets dark, pelican crossing lights that respond to a button being pushed and a kettle that turns off when the water boils.
✦ Explain how the outdoor light monitors movement and when this is detected it switches on the light (monitor – movement, control – light) and how the pelican crossing uses pressure from pressing the button to control the light and signal (monitor – pressure, control – lights and signal).
✦ Talk about why we need these things. Consider safety issues – the kettle turns itself off, the crossings tell us when it is safe to cross and it saves time having street lights turn on automatically. How long have we used such devices? Did our grandparents have access to them, for example?
✦ Ask the children to think about other devices that rely on control to make them work and whether the device works on a single instruction or a sequence of instructions.

(Make sure you read the safety guidelines that come with the control box before using it.)

 Group activities

Focus group – with the teacher

✦ Explain that a computer can be used to control things such as a light bulb when we use it together with special software and something called a control box.
✦ (This is an example for one type of control box. Read your own manual for instructions for your box.) Show the children the control box and how to plug a light bulb into output socket 1 by using the jack plug and wires attached to the bulb holder. (First ensure the bulbs are working and check that the voltage of the bulbs matches the control box.) Explain that the light can be switched on and off by writing instructions using control language (ie 'SWITCHON 1' turns the bulb on, 'SWITCHOFF 1' turns the bulb off). Explain how the command relates to the socket into which the device is plugged (socket 1). Make sure they understand that all three devices (bulb, control box and computer) must be joined to each other correctly before it will work. Demonstrate how to set up a procedure to flash the light and how to name the procedure, for example:

press BUILD (or relevant command)
type BULB (name of procedure) press return
SWITCHON 1 (return)
WAIT 50 (return)
SWITCHOFF 1 (return)
press escape
Then type BULB (return)

for flashing lights:
REPEAT 5
SWITCHON 1
WAIT 50
SWITCHOFF 1
END

✦ Ask the children to write their own procedures to flash a bulb. Ask them to record the results.

Using the photocopiable activity sheets

✦ Use the sheets after the computer session.

 Plenary session

Share the procedures the children recorded and tested. Discuss the importance of accuracy in the language used and in the use of timing. Discuss the consequences of each error in the diagrams on the activity sheets to reinforce the importance of correctly joining all the components.

✦ The control box ✦

✦ Here is a procedure to make a bulb light up and stay on for 5 seconds. One of the instructions is missing. Choose the missing instruction from those provided and write it in.

SWITCHON 1

_____

SWITCHOFF 1

Note: 5 seconds = WAIT 50

Choose from these instructions:

SWITCHON 2

WAIT 5

WAIT 50

SWITCHOFF 2

✦ Look at this diagram of a control box joined to a computer and a bulb. There is something wrong with the way it is connected. Put a circle around the mistake. Then write down why this would cause a problem.

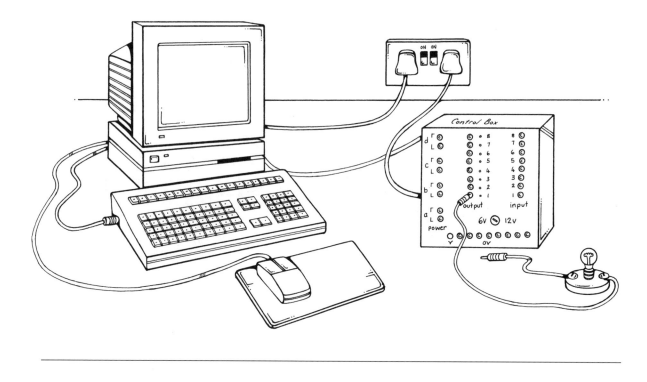

_____

_____

◆ The control box ◆

◆ Write the procedure for making a bulb light up and stay on for 10 seconds in socket 3 on the control box. Choose your instructions from those in the box.

_____

_____

_____

Note: 5 seconds = WAIT 50

Choose from these instructions:	
SWITCHON 2	WAIT 100
WAIT 5	SWITCHON 3
WAIT 50	SWITCHOFF 3
SWITCHOFF 2	WAIT 10

◆ Look at this diagram of a control box joined to a computer and a bulb. There are two things wrong with the way it is connected. Put a circle around the mistakes. Then write down why they would cause a problem.

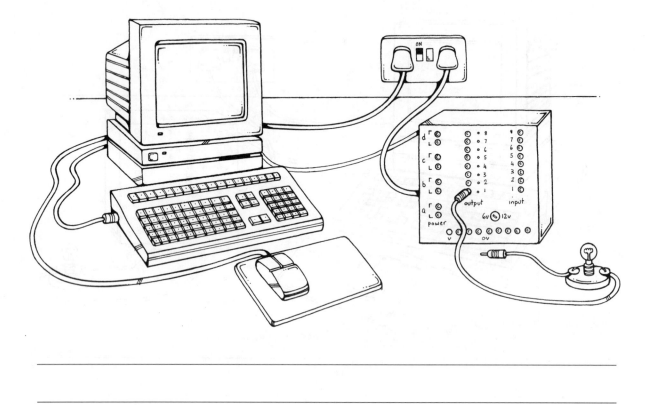

_____

_____

_____

✦ The control box ✦

✦ Write the procedure for making a light bulb flash on and off 6 times (for 5 seconds each) with a 2-second wait between them. Use the repeat command.

_____

_____

_____

_____

Note: 5 seconds = WAIT 50

_____

✦ Look at this diagram of a control box joined to a computer and a bulb. There are 3 things wrong with the way it is connected. Put a circle around the mistakes. Then write down why they would cause a problem.

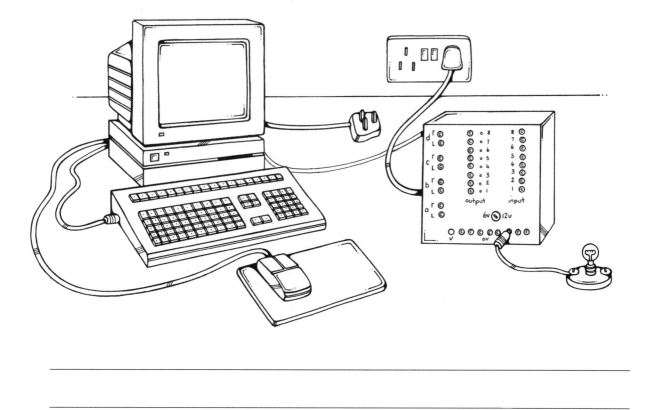

_____

_____

_____

Lesson 13

Controlling devices – 2

 Learning objectives

✦ To use simple procedures to control more than one output device.
✦ To use simple control language to activate multiple devices concurrently.

 Resources

✦ Control box and software that sends instructions from the computer to the control box.
✦ A model of some traffic lights made from a cardboard tube, coloured cellophane and small bulbs and bulb holders (see the diagram below).
✦ Jack plugs that fit the sockets on the control box.
✦ Insulated wire for connection to the bulbs.

 Whole class introduction

✦ Remind the children about the work they carried out in Lesson 12. Tell them that today they are going to make some traffic lights (unless you have ready-made ones). Show them a prepared model (such as below) and discuss the sequence of lights (red, red and amber, green).
✦ Ask them to work in pairs to write a procedure for each part of the light sequence. Explain that in order to turn on more than one output at a time (ie red and amber), they need to program two sockets to come on at once, for example:
    SWITCHON 3
    SWITCHON 2

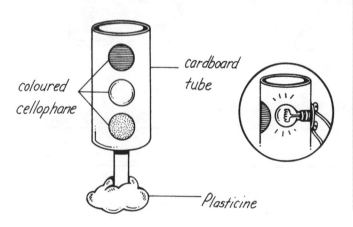

 Group activities

Focus group – with the teacher

✦ Ask each pair to test out their procedures using the computer and control box. Remind them to check that each component is connected correctly. Ask them to record any amendments they may need to make and to describe the results.
✦ Finally, ask them to write a repeat procedure to make the traffic light sequence go through several cycles. (Refer to your own manual.)

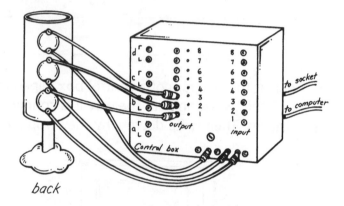

back

Using the photocopiable activity sheets

✦ Use the sheets after the computer session.

 Plenary session

Share the children's recordings from the computer session. What kinds of changes did they need to make to their original procedures? Why were these changes necessary? Discuss the activity sheets. How important is it for a set of traffic lights to work in the correct sequence? What safety implications are there? What would be the difference in the control of a set of ordinary traffic lights compared with pedestrian crossing ones where a button needs to be pushed before the sequence changes?

✦ Change it! ✦

✦ The Rosewood Home for the elderly has a pelican crossing outside it. Unfortunately the green light does not stay on long enough for the old people to get across the road. Change the procedure below to make the green light stay on longer (60 seconds).

```
SWITCHON 3
WAIT 500
SWITCHOFF 3
WAIT 10
SWITCHON 3
SWITCHON 2
WAIT 30
SWITCH OFF 3
SWITCHOFF 2
WAIT 10
SWITCHON 1
WAIT 100
SWITCHOFF 1
WAIT 20
```

Note:

red = socket No. 3

amber = socket No. 2

green = socket No. 1

WAIT 50 = 5 seconds

✦ The red traffic light on the model below is not wired up correctly. Change the wiring by crossing out the wire that is incorrectly connected. Redraw the correct wiring in red.

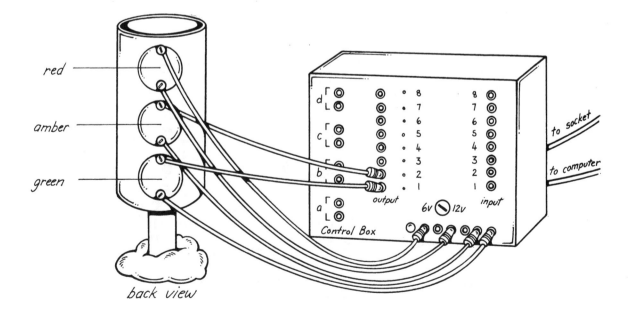

✦ Change it! ✦

✦ The local pelican crossing lights are faulty! Instead of red and amber coming on together, they show red and green! Also the green light only stays on for 10 seconds when it should be on for 60 seconds. Make the changes necessary to the procedure below.

SWITCHON 3
WAIT 500
SWITCHOFF 3
WAIT 10
SWITCHON 3
SWITCHON 1
WAIT 30
SWITCH OFF 3
SWITCHOFF 1
WAIT 10
SWITCHON 1
WAIT 100
SWITCHOFF 1
WAIT 20

Note:

red = socket 3

amber = socket 2

green = socket 1

WAIT 50 = 5 seconds

✦ Check the wiring below on this model traffic light. You should find two mistakes. Cross out anything that is wired incorrectly and redraw what it should be in red pen.

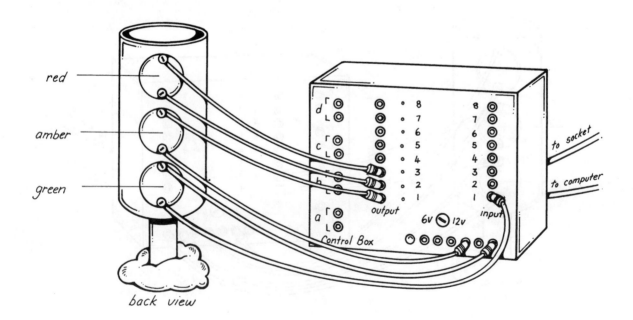

back view

✦ Change it! ✦

✦ The procedure for a set of traffic lights below has been written incorrectly. Rewrite it to correct all the errors and change the wait times for the red and green lights to 60 seconds each.

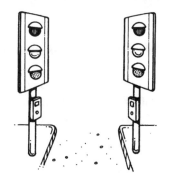

```
SWITCHON 3
WAIT 500
WAIT 10
SWITCHON 3
SWITCHON 1
WAIT 30
WAIT 10
SWITCHON 1
WAIT 100
SWITCHOFF 1
WAIT 20
```

Note:

red = socket 3

amber = socket 2

green = socket 1

WAIT 50 = 5 seconds

✦ The wiring on this model traffic light is incorrect. Change it by redrawing how it should be on the back of this page.

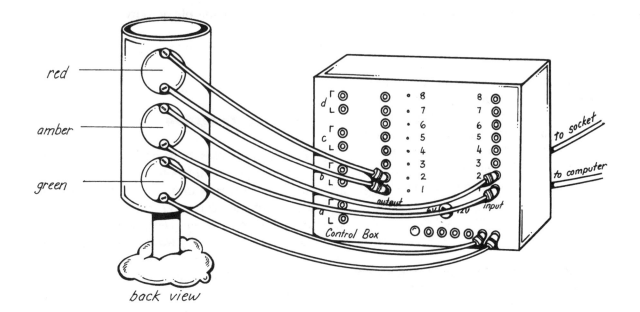

Lesson 14

Controlling devices – 3

Learning objectives

✦ To control output devices by building a sequence of events to solve a problem.
✦ To control a number of output devices.

Resources

✦ Control box and software that sends instructions from the computer to the control box.
✦ Jack plugs to fit the sockets on the control box.
✦ Small bulbs and bulb holders, buzzers, small motors and insulated wire.

Whole class introduction

✦ Discuss examples of control technology going wrong and the consequences of this. For example, 'What might happen if the bleeper on pelican crossings came on with the red light instead of the green one?' and 'What might happen if the streetlights did not come on when it got dark?' Talk also about how people can cope when technology goes wrong, for example when the fog warning signs on a motorway fail on a foggy day. Hopefully people are aware that they still need to slow down even when the warning signs are absent!
✦ Then go on to remind them how control technology has been developed to make our lives easier and better – how it can help us to be, for example, warmer (turning on central heating) and safer (automatic outdoor lighting). Then tell the children that they are going to design and make some control technology for a specific purpose – to help make someone's life better.

Group activities

✦ (You will need to refer to the manual for your own control box for the following activities.) Tell the children you want them to solve a problem for a fairground ride owner. He is very disappointed about the fact that people are not noticing the sign he has put up to advertise his ride. He has three ideas in mind:
Group 1 is to make a small sign from card with several lights around the edge of it. Write a procedure to make the lights flash on and off one after the other in quick succession.
Group 2 does the same as Group 1 but adds a buzzer to attract attention. The buzzer should go on and off after every second light flashes.
Group 3 does the same as Group 2 but adds a coloured wheel that spins around using a small motor.

✦ Ask the children to work in pairs or as a group to write the procedure and get any materials they need to make their model.

Focus group – with the teacher

✦ Ask the children to test out their models using the control box and computer. Help them to check for any errors in their procedures if the sequence does not work as planned and to record the changes they needed to make.

Using the photocopiable activity sheets

✦ The sheets can be used before or after the group activities.

Plenary session

Share the responses to the activity sheets – does everyone agree on the potential seriousness of each problem? How important is it that control devices function correctly? Discuss the tasks each group had to carry out. Did they have to alter their procedures in any way? How did this affect the results? What are the limitations of using these devices? Which sign do they think would be most effective for the fairground ride owner (Group 1, 2 or 3)? Why?

✦ When things go wrong! ✦

✦   The following is a set of examples of control technology going wrong. Decide how serious the problem is by ticking the appropriate box.

	not serious repair sometime	quite serious repair soon	very serious repair immediately
1. The bleeper on a pelican crossing fails to work but the green light is working correctly.	☐	☐	☐
2. The arm on a carpark barrier fails to work when the ticket is removed.	☐	☐	☐
3. Both sets of lights at a traffic intersection are showing green at the same time.	☐	☐	☐
4. An electric kettle fails to switch off when the water has boiled.	☐	☐	☐
5. The amber light does not come on in a set of traffic lights but red and green are working normally.	☐	☐	☐
6. A classroom heater fails to turn off at the end of the day.	☐	☐	☐
7. A pelican crossing fails to change to green when the button is pushed.	☐	☐	☐
8. Some party lights fail to flash on and off. They stay on all the time.	☐	☐	☐

✦   Now choose one of the examples that you think could be very serious and write down what you think might happen if the problem was not fixed.

✦ When things go wrong! ✦

✦ The following is a set of examples of control technology going wrong. Decide how serious each problem is.

not serious – repair sometime
fairly serious – repair soon
very serious – repair immediately

Then write down what you think could happen because of this problem.

1. The bleeper on a pelican crossing fails to work but the green light is working correctly.

_____
_____
_____
_____

2. The arm on a carpark barrier fails to work when the ticket is removed.

_____
_____
_____
_____

3. Both sets of lights at a traffic intersection are showing green at the same time.

_____
_____
_____
_____
_____

4. An electric kettle fails to switch off when the water has boiled.

_____
_____
_____
_____

5. The amber light does not come on in a set of traffic lights but red and green are working normally.

_____
_____
_____
_____

6. A classroom heater fails to turn off at the end of the day.

_____
_____
_____
_____

7. Some party lights fail to flash on and off. They stay on all the time.

_____
_____
_____

✦ When things go wrong! ✦

✦ The following is a set of examples of control technology going wrong. Decide how serious each problem is.

not serious – repair sometime
fairly serious – repair soon
very serious – repair immediately

Write down what you think could happen because of this problem. Then say what you think may have gone wrong in the procedure when programming it. The first one has been done for you.

1. The bleeper on a pelican crossing fails to work but the green light is working correctly.

Very serious for blind people who would not know when to cross the road safely. The bleeper has not been programmed to switch on and off at the same time as the green light.

2. The arm on a carpark barrier fails to work when the ticket is removed.

_____
_____
_____
_____

3. Both sets of lights at a traffic intersection are showing green at the same time.

_____
_____
_____
_____

4. An electric kettle fails to switch off when the water has boiled.

_____
_____
_____
_____
_____

5. The amber light does not come on in a set of traffic lights but red and green are working normally.

_____
_____
_____
_____

6. A classroom heater fails to turn off at the end of the day.

_____
_____
_____
_____

✦ Appendix ✦

 Suggestions for using these pages...

Page 63

✦ This page is used with Lesson 1. Enlarge it on a photocopier if required.

Page 64

✦ This page is used with Lesson 2. Enlarge it on a photocopier if required.
✦ The children could use the plan to stimulate ideas for planning a 'dream' home. They could draw the rooms using the drawing package and glue the print-out onto a large sheet of paper. They could then cut out pictures of furniture from magazines together with fabric and wallpaper samples to attach around the border of the plan to present as a designer's drawing.

Page 65

✦ This page is used with Lesson 3. Photocopy enough pages for each child to have one card each. Cut them out.

Page 66

✦ This page is used with Lesson 4. Enlarge it on a photocopier. Cut the page in half to separate the record cards from the graph.
✦ The record cards can also be used with Lesson 5.

Page 67

✦ This page is used with Lesson 6. Enlarge it on a photocopier if required.
✦ The children could carry out their own searches about Manchester using a CD-Rom or the Internet to compare the information.
✦ An interesting geography/history project could be carried out comparing the English places with American ones of the same name.

Page 68

✦ This page is used with Lessons 7 and 8. Enlarge it on a photocopier if required.

✦ The children could make up stories or reports based on the information on each person in the survey – who is Kylie Jeffs? What is she really like? The writing could be word-processed and presented as a class book.

Page 69

✦ This page is used with Lesson 8. Enlarge it on a photocopier if required. Cut out the four separate graphs and charts.
✦ The children could measure their own heights and the hourly temperature to make comparative graphs and charts.

Page 70

✦ This page is used with Lessons 9 and 10. Enlarge it on a photocopier or copy it out onto the board.

Page 71

✦ This page is used with Lesson 11. Enlarge it on a photocopier or copy it out onto the board.

Answers to Lesson 8

Activity sheet 1

1 (11.03) 12.00	should be 11.30
2 12.00 = 18 degrees	should be around 14-15
3 semi-detached = 25%	should be 50%
4 Lucy = 150mm	should be 150cm

Activity sheet 2

1 11.30 (12.05)	should be 12.15
2 13.00 = 10 degrees	should be around 16
3 semi-detached = 65%	should be 75%
4 Sara = 156m	should be 1.56m

Activity sheet 3

1 16.20 (17.45)	should be 17.55
2 Tues 13.00 = 10 degrees	should be around 14
3 detached = 35.5%	should be 37.5%
4 Sara = 156m	should be 1.56m
	average should be 1.54m

ICT Skills

✦ Manipulating shapes ✦

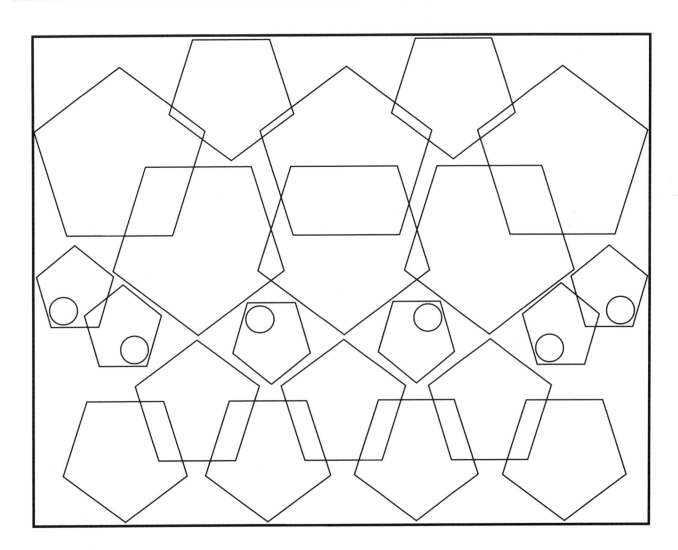

Translation: changing an object's position by sliding it without turning.

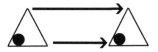

Rotation: changing an object's position by turning it about a fixed point through a given angle.

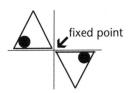

Reflection: a mirror image of an object.

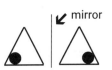

ICT Skills
Year 5/P6

ICT
Skills

Photocopiable
©Hopscotch Educational Publishing

63

✦ Plans ✦

Side and plan views of kitchen objects:

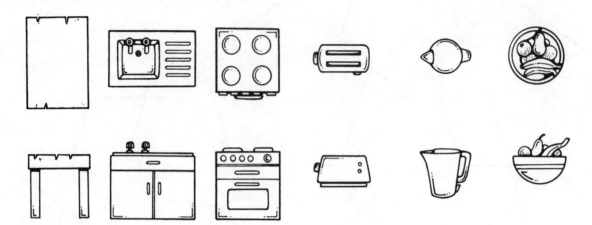

Kitchen plan:

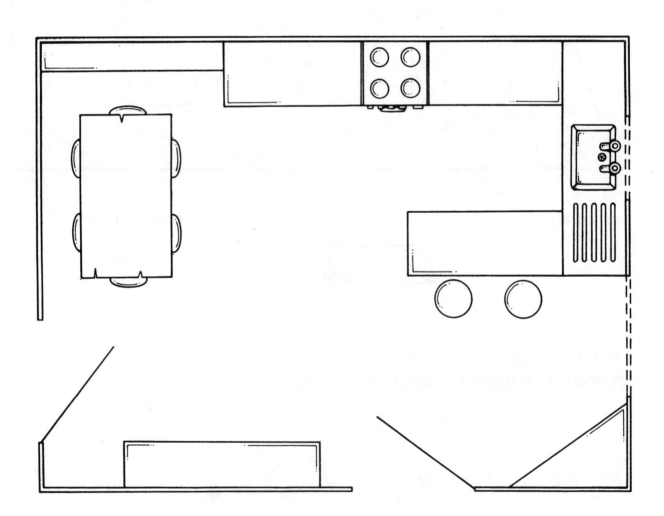

ICT Skills

✦ Record cards ✦

Name: Age: No. of brothers or sisters: Eye colour: Hair colour: Travel to school (walk, car, cycle, bus): Favourite sport: Do you play a sport?	Name: Age: No. of brothers or sisters: Eye colour: Hair colour: Travel to school (walk, car, cycle, bus): Favourite sport: Do you play a sport?
Name: Age: No. of brothers or sisters: Eye colour: Hair colour: Travel to school (walk, car, cycle, bus): Favourite sport: Do you play a sport?	Name: Age: No. of brothers or sisters: Eye colour: Hair colour: Travel to school (walk, car, cycle, bus): Favourite sport: Do you play a sport?
Name: Age: No. of brothers or sisters: Eye colour: Hair colour: Travel to school (walk, car, cycle, bus): Favourite sport: Do you play a sport?	Name: Age: No. of brothers or sisters: Eye colour: Hair colour: Travel to school (walk, car, cycle, bus): Favourite sport: Do you play a sport?
Name: Age: No. of brothers or sisters: Eye colour: Hair colour: Travel to school (walk, car, cycle, bus): Favourite sport: Do you play a sport?	Name: Age: No. of brothers or sisters: Eye colour: Hair colour: Travel to school (walk, car, cycle, bus): Favourite sport: Do you play a sport?

ICT Skills
Year 5/P6

ICT
Skills

Photocopiable
©Hopscotch Educational Publishing

65

✦ Birds ✦

name: fulmar   1
land/sea: sea
colour: silver-grey, white
food: fish
wingspan: 34cm   **body length:** 47cm
egg colour: white
max no. of eggs laid: 1
nest site: cliffs

name: barn owl   2
land/sea: land
colour: white, buff
food: small rodents
wingspan: 29cm   **body length:** 34cm
egg colour: white
max no. of eggs laid: 8
nest site: buildings

name: greenfinch   3
land/sea: land
colour: yellow-green
food: seeds
wingspan: 9cm   **body length:** 15cm
egg colour: white, red/brown spots
max no. of eggs laid: 6
nest site: trees, hedges

name: starling   4
land/sea: land
colour: black, iridescent green/purple
food: insects, fruit
wingspan: 13cm   **body length:** 22cm
egg colour: pale blue
max no. of eggs laid: 7
nest site: holes in trees, buildings

name: peregrine falcon   5
land/sea: land
colour: grey-brown, buff
food: birds
wingspan: 35cm   **body length:** 48cm
egg colour: orange-red, brown
max no. of eggs laid: 4
nest site: ledges, cliffs

name: robin   6
land/sea: land
colour: red, brown
food: worms, insects, fruit, seeds
wingspan: 8cm   **body length:** 14cm
egg colour: white, speckled
max no. of eggs laid: 6
nest site: holes in walls, trees

name: puffin   7
land/sea: sea
colour: black, white
food: fish
wingspan: 18cm   **body length:** 30cm
egg colour: white with faint spots
max no. of eggs laid: 1
nest site: holes, burrows

name: raven   8
land/sea: land
colour: black
food: birds, mammals, dead animals
wingspan: 40cm   **body length:** 64cm
egg colour: blue-green, speckled
max no. of eggs laid: 7
nest site: rock ledges

name: house sparrow   9
land/sea: land
colour: brown
food: seeds, insects
wingspan: 7cm   **body length:** 14cm
egg colour: cream, speckled
max no. of eggs laid: 6
nest site: buildings, hedges

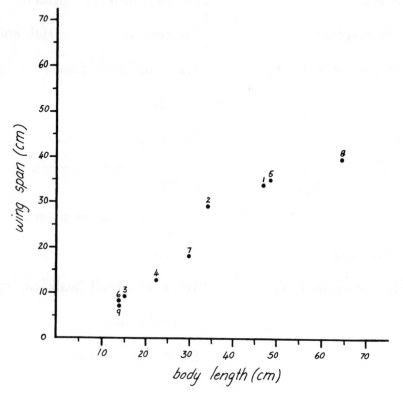

ICT Skills

✦ Manchester ✦

- ● History
- ● How to get there
- ● Places of interest
- ● Leisure
- ● Library

Manchester

museums page

home

hotels

Manchester, a small city in Hartford County, Central Connecticut, lies on the Hockanum River, near Hartford. It was settled in 1672 and was incorporated in 1823. Manchester manufactures precision tools, textiles, parachutes and aerospace equipment. There is an excellent school system and a Community-Technical College.

Located near the center of the town is a historic district that has many buildings from the town's early years, including a restored 1901 firehouse (now a museum) and a 1751 schoolhouse. There is also a glass works and a children's museum.

Population (1980) 49 761; (1990) 51 618

This site developed and maintained by Manchester Technologies.

last update: August 1999

The firehouse, now a museum

The town hall, 41 Center Street

Manchester art galleries

Manchester

Museum of science and industry

Manchester, a city in the north west and administrative centre of Greater Manchester, lies on the Irwell, Medlock, Irk and Tib rivers. Manchester is a major industrial centre and port. It produces cotton, paper, pharmaceuticals, electrical and aircraft equipment, computers and food products.

Educational establishments include the Victoria University of Manchester, the Royal Northern College of Music and a polytechnic college. Museums include: archaeology, natural history and science and technology.

The city suffered a lot of damage from bombing during World War II but has since undergone extensive rebuilding. Population (1991 estimate) 432 600.

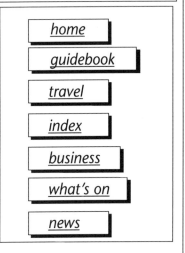

home
guidebook
travel
index
business
what's on
news

This is the official website for Manchester. Last update Sept 1994.

✦ Spot the mistakes! ✦

Here is the information collected from a questionnaire conducted in January 2000 by *Teen-Scene Clothing*, a company specialising in clothing for boys and girls aged between 13 and 16.

Name: Iqbal Aslam **DOB:** 15. 3. 85 **Male/female:** male **Height:** 160 cm **Chest:** 87cm **Waist:** 70 cm **Favourite colour:** blue	**Name:** Julia Robins **DOB:** 2. 11. 87 **Male/female:** female **Height:** 1.68 cm **Chest:** 85 cm **Waist:** 68 cm **Favourite colour:** blue	**Name:** Emma Johnson **DOB:** 28. 8. 86 **Male/female:** female **Height:** 165 cm **Chest:** 90 cm **Waist:** 70 cm **Favourite colour:** red	**Name:** Ranjit Singh **DOB:** 1. 12. 85 **Male/female:** male **Height:** 168 cm **Chest:** 91 cm **Waist:** 75 cm **Favourite colour:** green
Name: Ann Simnel **DOB:** 25. 7. 86 **Male/female:** female **Height:** 167 cm **Chest:** 87cm **Waist:** 73 cm **Favourite colour:** red	**Name:** Sara James **DOB:** 1. 9. 87 **Male/female:** girl **Height:** 156 cm **Chest:** 82 cm **Waist:** 68 cm **Favourite colour:** white	**Name:** Claire Wright **DOB:** 5. 10. 82 **Male/female:** female **Height:** 168 cm **Chest:** 90 cm **Waist:** 74 cm **Favourite colour:** red	**Name:** Jean Rowle **DOB:** 8. 4. 85 **Male/female:** female **Height:** 154 cm **Chest:** 85cm **Waist:** 6.7cm **Favourite colour:** blue
Name: Maya Ensio **DOB:** 6. 12. 87 **Male/female:** female **Height:** 154 cm **Chest:** 83cm **Waist:** 68 cm **Favourite colour:** purple	**Name:** Tamsen Rogers **DOB:** 5. 3. 87 **Male/female:** female **Height:** 158 cm **Chest:** 85 cm **Waist:** 70 cm **Favourite colour:** blue	**Name:** Lisa Michaels **DOB:** 1. 6. 85 **Male/female:** female **Height:** 170 cm **Chest:** 87cm **Waist:** seventy cm **Favourite colour:** black	**Name:** Kylie Jeffs **DOB:** 11. 10. 87 **Male/female:** female **Height:** 162 cm **Chest:** 87cm **Waist:** 65 cm **Favourite colour:** gold
Name: Angela Smith **DOB:** 7. 7. 87 **Male/female:** female **Height:** 155 cm **Chest:** 83 cm **Waist:** 65 cm **Favourite colour:** green	**Name:** Michelle Little **DOB:** 24. 5. 85 **Male/female:** female **Height:** 172 cm **Chest:** 9.1cm **Waist:** 70 cm **Favourite colour:** black	**Name:** Lena White **DOB:** 25. 3. 86 **Male/female:** female **Height:** 171 cm **Chest:** 88 cm **Waist:** 74 cm **Favourite colour:** red	**Name:** Helen Moss **DOB:** 4. 11. 85 **Male/female:** female **Height:** 170 cm **Chest:** 90 cm **Waist:** 71 cm **Favourite colour:** black
Name: Olivia Speak **DOB:** 2. 8. 84 **Male/female:** female **Height:** 173 cm **Chest:** 88 cm **Waist:** 67 cm **Favourite colour:** blue	**Name:** Imogen Ford **DOB:** 20. 12. 85 **Male/female:** female **Height:** 170 cm **Chest:** 91cm **Waist:** 73 cm **Favourite colour:** black	**Name:** Sharon Rock **DOB:** 16. 13. 86 **Male/female:** female **Height:** 173 cm **Chest:** 87 cm **Waist:** 75 cm **Favourite colour:** blue	**Name:** Hyjinta Merlon **DOB:** 5. 1. 87 **Male/female:** female **Height:** 155 cm **Chest:** 80 cm **Waist:** 62 cm **Favourite colour:** red

ICT Skills

Photocopiable
©Hopscotch Educational Publishing

Height of children in survey

Name		Height
1	Iqbal	160 cm
2	Julia	1.68cm
3	Emma	165 cm
4	Ranjit	168 cm
5	Ann	167 cm
6	Sara	156 cm
7	Claire	168 cm
8	Jean	154 cm
9	Maya	154 cm
10	Tamsen	158 cm
11	Lisa	170 cm
12	Kylie	162 cm
13	Angela	155 cm
14	Michelle	172 cm
15	Lena	171 cm
16	Helen	170 cm
17	Olivia	173 cm
18	Imogen	170 cm
19	Sharon	173 cm
20	Hyjinta	155 cm

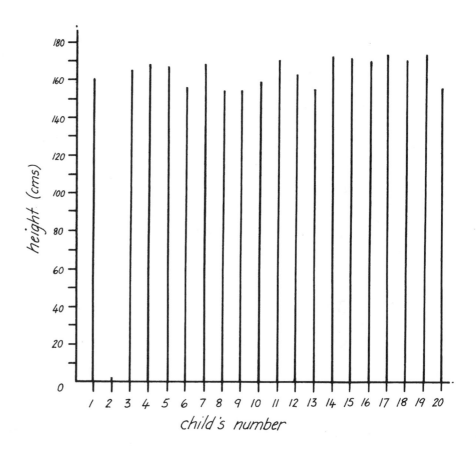

shortest person = 154 cm
tallest person = 173 cm
average height = 156 cm

Hourly Temperatures – Wednesday

Time	Temperature
9.00	14 $^{\circ}$C
10.00	15 $^{\circ}$C
11.00	16 $^{\circ}$C
12.00	18 $^{\circ}$C
13.00	18 $^{\circ}$C
14.00	10 $^{\circ}$C
15.00	18 $^{\circ}$C
16.00	17 $^{\circ}$C
17.00	17 $^{\circ}$C

Hourly Temperatures – Wednesday

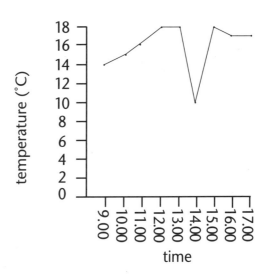

✦ Holiday budgeting ✦

	A	B	C	D	E
1	*item*				
2	taxi to airport				
3	flight				
4	villa				
5	food				
6	spending money				
7	taxi home				
8	insurance				
9	*total*				

taxi to airport
£30.00 each way

flight
£149.00 each person
over 2 years of age

villa (per week)
up to 2 adults – £200.00
family – £400.00

holiday insurance

insurance (up to 7 days):
1 adult = £15.95
family = £39.95

insurance (up to 14 days):
1 adult = £16.95
family = £42.95

ICT Skills

Photocopiable
©Hopscotch Educational Publishing

◆ Aeropark ◆

	A	B	C	D
1	day	adults	children	total
2	Monday	105	220	
3	Tuesday	220	454	
4	Wednesday	268	525	
5	Thursday	220	489	
6	Friday	325	784	
7	Saturday	795	1654	
8	Sunday	645	1827	
9	total			

1. total number of adults for week:

B9 = B2 + B3 + B4 + B5 + B6 + B7 + B8

= _____

2. total number of children for week:

C9 = C2 + C3 + C4 + C5 + C6 + C7 + C8

= _____

3. how many more children on Saturday than Monday?

C9 = C7 – C2

= _____

4. total number of people on Saturday:

D7 = B7 + C7

= _____

5. total number of people on Monday:

D2 = B2 + C2

= _____

6. how many more children than adults on Saturday?

D7 = C7 – B7

= _____

7. total number of people on Sunday:

D8 = B8 + C8

= _____

8. total number of people for week:

D9 = B9 + C9

= _____

Name_____ Year_____ Date_____ Level_____

Tick the boxes and look for best fit when assessing level.

QCA Expectations		QCA SoW Unit		NC level
some children will not have made so much progress and will:	use an object-based graphics package to create and manipulate basic objects	5A	☐	3
	carry out searches using two or more criteria	5B	☐	
	recognise the importance of checking data and that poor quality information leads to unreliable results	5C	☐	
	use a spreadsheet to produce a table of data	5D	☐	
	design and create a simple advertising display which produces a limited number of events; need help to write simple procedures and design the display	5E	☐	
most children will:	use an object-based graphics package to create, combine and manipulate objects and explore possibilities	5A	☐	4
	use 'AND', 'OR', '=<' and '=>' in their searches	5B	☐	
	interpret, check and question data; recognise that poor quality information leads to unreliable results	5C	☐	
	use a spreadsheet to carry out calculations	5D	☐	
	design and create a simple advertising display which produces a combination of events; write simple procedures and be able to link output devices together; amend their procedures to get a desired outcome	5E	☐	
some children will have progressed further and will:	use an object-based graphics package to create and explore an accurate graphical model checking predictions and make decisions	5A	☐	4-5
	carry out complex searches to check hypotheses	5B	☐	
	interpret, check and question data; use logical inference to identify implausible and inaccurate data; recognise that poor quality information leads to unreliable results	5C	☐	
	use a spreadsheet to carry out calculations; explore the effects of changing the data in a spreadsheet	5D	☐	
	design and create an imaginative advertising display which produces a combination of events; write, correct and improve procedures to link output devices together; realise the limitations of the system	5E	☐	

ICT Skills